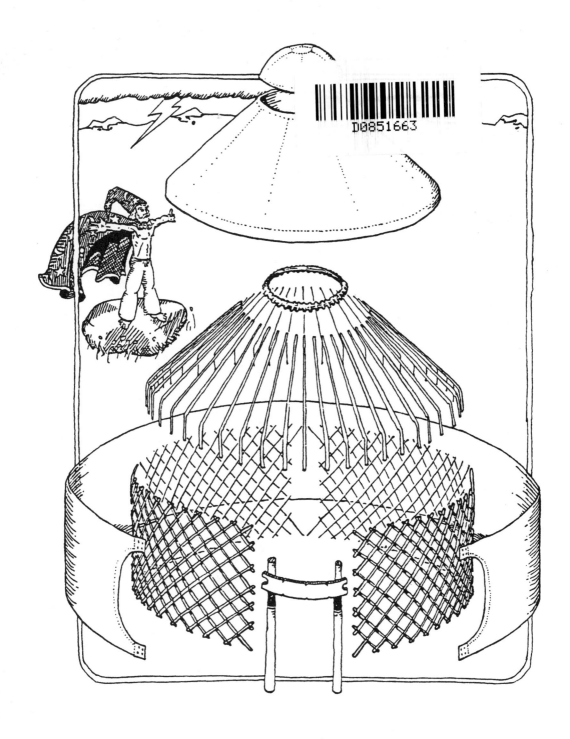

A Love Letter

With a circle one meter
You sit, pray and sing.

With a shelter ten meters large
You sleep well, rain sounds a lullaby.

With a field a hundred meters large
Grow rice, raise goats.

With a valley a thousand meters large
gather firewood, water, wild vegetables
                                     and Amanitas.

With a forest ten kilometers large
Play with raccoons, hawks
Poison snakes and butterflies.

Mountainous country Shinano
A hundred kilometers large
Where someone lives leisurely, they say.

Within a circle ten thousand kilometers large
Go to see the southern coral reef in summer
Or winter drifting ices in Ohotsuku.

Within a circle ten thousand kilometers large
Walking somewhere on the earth.

Within a circle one hundred thousand kilometers large
Swimming in the sea of shooting stars.

Within a circle a million kilometers large
Upon the spaced-out yellow rape blossoms
The moon in the east, the sun west.

Within a circle ten billion kilometers large
Pop far out of the solar system mandala.

Within a circle ten thousand light years large
The galaxy full blooming in spring.

Within a circle one billion light years large
Andromeda is melting away into snowing cherry
                                    flowers.

Now within a circle ten billion light years large
All thoughts of time, space are burnt away
And there again you sit, pray and sing
You sit, pray and sing.

                    Nanao
                    Sinano, Japan
                    May, 1976.

MONGOLIAN CLOUD HOUSES

How to make a Yurt and live Comfortably

By DAN FRANK KUEHN

Distributed in the United States and Canada by Publishers Group West.

Library of Congress Cataloging-in-Publication Data
Kuehn, Dan Frank, 1951–
    Mongolian cloud houses : how to make a yurt and live comfortably / by Dan Frank Kuehn.
        p.   cm.
    Includes bibliographical references
    ISBN-10: 0-936070-39-0
    ISBN-13: 978-0-936070-39-1
  1. Yurts—Design and construction.   2. Kuehn, Dan Frank, 1951– Homes and haunts.
I. Title.

TH4870.K84 2006
690′.879—dc22

                                                                        2006002839

10 9 8 7 6 5 4 3 2 1 — 10 09 08 07 06
(Lowest digits indicate number and year of latest printing.)

Printed in the United States of America

Donn P. Crane illustrations © The United Educators, Inc.
All other illustrations are by the author.
The calligraphy is by Nanao Sakaki.

Additional copies of this book may be purchased at your favorite bookstore or call for current pricing:

Shelter Publications, Inc.
P. O. Box 279
Bolinas, California 94924
Tel: 415-868-0280
Email: shelter@shelterpub.com
Orders, toll-free: 1-800-307-0131

Visit Our Website
SHELTER ONLINE
www.shelterpub.com

To Mom & Dad
and
to the wild child spirit of Ric Paulden

Contents

Introduction

I discovered yurts in the 1970s in Taos, New Mexico. In those years, Taos was a haven for free-thinking, artistic people. Innovative building methods were not only tolerated, but encouraged by the multicultural community that had sprung up in that unique part of the world. A friend of mine, Richard Peisenger, aka Sassafras, had built a 16-foot-diameter yurt of milled lath, held together with bolts and wingnuts, and covered with nylon-reinforced vinyl. I liked the spaciousness of the circle, the simplicity of design, and the concept of portability. I decided to build a smaller yurt—more practical for one guy, easier to heat—out of canvas, covering a lighter frame.

I started browsing through old *National Geographic* magazines, looking at the *gers* (yurts) built by Mongolian nomads in the Gobi Desert, trying to figure out how they were constructed. How did they do that? I was envisioning a yurt built for a slightly less severe climate than the Gobi. Then I ran across a full-sized *ger* with all the trappings in an exhibition at the Denver Museum of Art, and I was on my way.

My Yurt-Living Years

I started building yurts, and after living for three summers and then two complete years in homemade yurts at a dozen locations in Northern New Mexico I decided to write a book on building my most recent effort—a 13-foot-diameter yurt, framed with Johnson Grass (a bamboo-like plant, harvested 125 miles south of Taos, in Albuquerque), held together with rubber bands cut out of old inner tubes, and covered with natural canvas. The design was based on the status of my assets then: a lot of time, and very little money. The only cash I needed was for canvas, needles and thread, safety pins, and waterproofing: a total of about $175. The rest was gleaned from the woods, backyards, and the local dump.

In addition to the economy of this design, I liked the portability. Once the collapsible frame was complete, the yurt could be assembled in an hour, and taken apart even more quickly. The longest poles were about 8 feet long, making a compact load for any vehicle. Finding a place to erect it was never a problem. Owners of vacant land often liked the idea of a live-in caretaker, especially in a temporary structure that could be easily removed, leaving no tell-tale traces.

First Edition of *Mongolian Cloud Houses*

In 1980 I wrote and self-published 500 copies of *Mongolian Cloud Houses*, a name created by poet Lawrence Ferlinghetti. It described construction of the yurt I was living in at the very same time. Shortly after its self-publication, I moved to Maui.

In the 25 years (!) since, several things happened:

1. I continued my yurt research. Adventurous builders (alas, not I) had travelled to Mongolia and studied with actual *ger* craftsmen. Englishman Paul King studied Mongolian yurt building first-hand and had written a wonderful book, *The Complete Yurt Handbook*. It answered many questions I'd had for years *(see p. 128)*.

2. I decided to build another yurt in Hawaii, heavily influenced by Paul's research.

3. Shelter Publications contacted me about reprinting *Mongolian Cloud Houses*, to which I agreed.

The New Edition

A funny thing happened on the way to what seemed to be a simple reprint job of the original book: a ton of valuable new (and old) information on yurts had surfaced in the past two decades and we felt we couldn't leave it out of the book. So just what is this book?

This book describes how to build a yurt, and is intended for the individual who has lots of time but not much money. Many materials are scrounged for free (rubber inner tubes), or gleaned from nature (willow sticks). New updates to the book show alternative materials (bamboo) and new techniques that you could incorporate into your own personal take on the form. The Appendix contains a wealth of information we've assembled on yurt designs, ready-to-erect yurts available from a wide variety of manufacturers, plus tools, material suppliers, yurt books, videos, and photos. Throughout the book, we show alternative ways of doing things. On pp. 122–126 are old drawings by Donn P. Crane depicting the life of Genghis Khan. There are tips in "Other Ways" (pp. 31–45) on putting your yurt together. On pp. 88–91 you can learn about keeping clean in the woods by building a sweat lodge. The yurt and sweat lodge are from opposite sides of the globe, but the sweat became such a part of my life in the yurt that I felt this book would be incomplete without it.

In the last part of the book are references to yurt companies (if you're inclined to buy a readymade yurt), information on yurt-building supplies, and books on yurt building.

This Book Is Alive

Mongolian Cloud Houses grew over a five-year period when I was already living very simply. Rough drafts and final drawings were completed while living in my yurt. This book is alive, extending beyond its cover.

Check *CloudHouses.com* for an ongoing discussion of the expanding world-wide yurt culture, and related resources. There are many new and old ways to try out, many variations on the basic design to explore, and many, many more luxury extras to discover, relish, and share.

Online, I'll include more ideas and helpful hints from my own nomad experience, and from yours, too. If you have any tips you'd like to see included, please send them in via the web site, *CloudHouses.com*.

"A nomad I will remain for life,
in love with distant and uncharted places."
–Isabelle Eberhardt

"Two humans in friendship are stronger than walls of stone."
–saying represented on the flag of Mongolia

Thanks,
DAN FRANK KUEHN

GER VARIATIONS

"YARANGA"

"EVENK"

"CHAPARI"

"TELEUTI"

"SAGAITSI"

"ALACHIGH"

"TURKIC"

"TURKMEN"

"KAZAK"

"MONGOL"

"ALTAI-KIZHI"

"KIZILTSI"

"YOMUT"

"BARK GER"

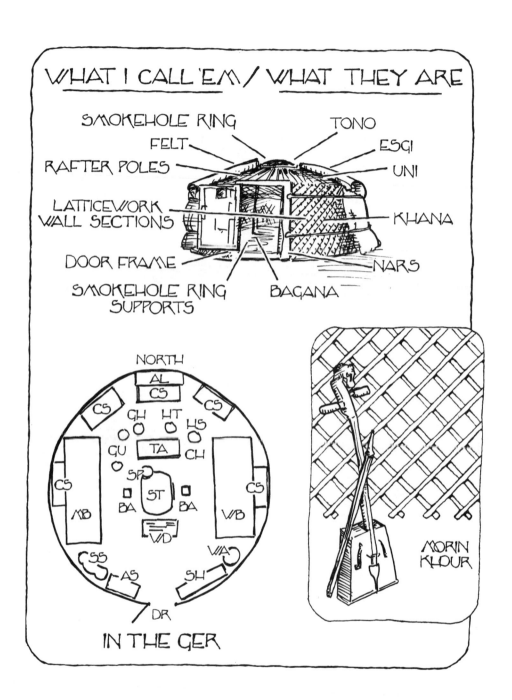

WHAT I CALL 'EM / WHAT THEY ARE

SMOKEHOLE RING — TONO

FELT — ESGI

RAFTER POLES — UNI

LATTICEWORK WALL SECTIONS — KHANA

DOOR FRAME — NARS

SMOKEHOLE RING SUPPORTS — BAGANA

NORTH

AL
CS
CS · CS
GH HT
GU   TA   HS · CH
CS   SP   CS
MB   BA ST BA   WB
VD
SS   WA
AS   SH
DR

IN THE GER

MORIN KHOUR

1
OLD WAYS

Nomadic sheep and yak herding communities migrate from the mountains to the plains in the fall, and back to the mountains in the spring, following the grass for their grazing animals. Over the course of a year, a *ger* may be moved as many as nine times, in a lifestyle that enables these people to thrive in the farthest reaches of Outer Mongolia, where even the summers are cold.

One to five camels or oxen will carry a collapsed *ger* and all its furnishings, depending on the size of the family. It's said that in Genghis Khan's day, huge *gers* (over 20 feet in diameter) were pulled, fully assembled on wheeled platforms, across the Gobi Desert by twenty or more oxen. *(See p. 126.)* Truly a mobile home!

The Russian word "yurt" has become the most common word these days to describe this structure. To the Mongols, the word *ger* simply means home, and for centuries these tents have been their only homes. They wouldn't have it any other way. In this book, I'll use the word *"ger"* to describe the original nomadic tents from Central Asia, and "yurt" for all others, copied, redesigned, or inspired from the original *ger*.

The basic parts of the *ger* have been called many things, but they already have other beautiful names *(opposite, above)*. Be advised, there doesn't seem to be a standardized way of spelling Mongolian words.

Legend for Illustration on Opposite Page

GU	Guests	**ST**	Stove
GH	Guest of honor	**SP**	Stovepipe
HT	Host	**WD**	Fuel—wood, dung, etc.
HS	Hostess	**SH**	Shelves—cooking
WB	Women's bed	**WA**	Water
CH	Children	**SA**	Saddle stand
MB	Men's bed	**AS**	Airag bag on stand
CS	Chests—storage	**BA**	Bagana—roof supports
AL	Altar	**DR**	Door
TA	Low table for serving		

The interior arrangement of the *ger* is fairly consistent in Asian culture. The door faces south. At the rear is the altar, with the men's area on the left side and the women's and children's on the right, everyone sleeping with their heads toward the altar.

The fire or stove (the stove's door facing the women's bed) is in the center and a low table, between the fire and the altar, is for serving. Honored guests sit between the men's side and the altar. Just inside the door, to the left, are the men's saddles and equipment along with a bag of fermented mare's milk. To the right of the door are the cooking area, food, sewing machine, etc.

The life of the Central Asian nomads seems romantic. Self-sufficient and independent, with elegantly decorated *gers* and clothes, they follow the seasonal grazing, with yaks and camels and horses, and their home, the *ger*. These people are fiercely independent, and have lived their lives on their own terms for countless generations across unimaginably vast, unfenced landscapes.

All true, but the climate is harsh and the people living this way must be hardy.

- The main diet is meat and milk products, supplemented with grain when they have it. Fresh fruit and green vegetables are rarely eaten.

- Food is cooked over a small stove, burning wood or dung cakes. *(See p. 12.)*

- The Mongols' horses are descendants of the world's oldest wild horses, but there is no need to tie them, for they always stay close to camp.

- Popular sports are horsemanship, wrestling, and a kind of polo that's played with the carcass of a goat.

- Sex roles in this part of the world are very defined. Women are the housekeepers and child-raisers and men the providers.

Despite efforts to suppress their way of life and put them on communes, the Mongolian nomadic tribes have been more successful than most natives at resisting change, probably because they are constantly on the move. Even now, semi-permanent yurts, equipped with gas heat and electricity, comprise many of the suburbs of Ulaanbaatar.

The Traditional Yurt

While this book deals mostly with one particular yurt, my home for a few years in the 70's, here we'll look at some time-honored features of the original cloud houses in enough detail that you could exchange them with those of my models and come up with your own unique versions.

Across Asia, as in the western world, you'll find many variations in the basic *ger* design. I've seen photos of wall-less *gers* (*left below,* like wide tipis with smokeholes), and wooden six-sided yurts in Siberia, with diameters from a 10-foot herder's *ger* to a huge (at least 30-foot) Buddhist priests' reception *ger*. At right below is another *ger*, also huge, with three stories like a wedding cake. There are smoky *gers* with dung fires, and modern Mongolian prefab *gers* with solar panels and satellite dishes (*p. 139*).

Traditional Bones

The usual building material for the *ger* framework is wood — young saplings from willow, poplar, hazel, or some other straight-growing tree. The yurts I've built have all had frames made from Johnson grass, found in the Albuquerque area, and more recently, using bamboo varieties, which grew where I was living in Hawaii at the time.

The thickness of the poles is determined by the size of the yurt, with larger yurts having stouter poles. Green wood can be straightened or curved using the heat-and-bend system outlined below (*see p. 21*) or fastened onto a properly shaped form to dry.

See p. 33 for more ideas.

One way to initially straighten solid wooden poles is to tie them tightly into a bundle while they're still green, carefully aligning each pole, as shown here. When the bundle is dry, the poles will keep their new shape.

TRADITIONAL BONES

A
1.
2.
3.

B

C
1.
2.

Rivets

The "rivet" connection *(A-1, at left)* used on the *khana,* or latticework wall sections, is made by first drilling small holes (about ⅛") at each of the intersections. Wet rawhide, still used these days, is knotted at one end, threaded through both poles, and knotted again. *(See p. 6.)*

The Rafters

Rafter poles have two holes near the bottom end, threaded with a loop of cord that hooks over the inside leg of each top "X" around the wall *(A-2)*. Often seen is a brightly colored woven band wrapped once around each rafter, part or all the way around the roof frame, 1 to 2 feet above the wall/roof junction *(A-3)*.

Nars – The Door

The solid wooden door, often a double door, is set in a solid wooden doorframe, with a felt or cloth second door. The wood door is strong, closes tightly to keep out the wind, and can be locked.

Usually made without nails, the pieces fit ingeniously into each other *(B)*. The "trunnion" door hinge is simply dowels extending from the top and bottom of one side of the door that fit into the holes in the door frame. The holes on the sides and top of the door frame are for fastening the wall and rafter poles. Often, there are also metal loops for tying the horsehair ropes that circle the *ger,* securing the felt and canvas cover.

The Smokehole Ring

The smokehole ring, the crown, or *tono,* is the most important single piece of the *ger,* and its construction is left to skilled craftsmen. At the center and top of the *ger,* it represents a portal to heaven.

This smokehole ring *(C)* is drawn after a homemade, somewhat primitive one I saw in an old *National Geographic*. A stick dome framework is built into the ring, so that a heavy blanket or tarp can cover it. This ring has square holes, for squared *uni* ends.

The *tono* is made in two layers of four sections each, with the second layer of four sections laid on top to cross the seams of the first layer, making a solid ring 2 to 3 feet in diameter. There are plans for a similar smokehole ring in "Bones II," at the end of this chapter.

A less severe roof angle than mine will be noted in most Mongolian yurts. The Mongols, especially on the vast flat Gobi Desert, have to deal with high winds, not the deep snow and penetrating rains of warmer climates.

A

B

TRADITIONAL
SKIN

Traditional Skin

Felt

The most common *ger* covering has always been felt made from sheep wool, with cotton canvas appearing both as an inside and outside layer, to protect the felt.

Felt is much easier and faster to produce by hand than woven cloth and is wind- and water-resistant. If you're interested in yurts and live in an area with high winds and very cold temperatures, you might consider a felt yurt. Like living in a wool sweater, felt can be cozy on a cold day.

Drawbacks of felt as a yurt covering include weight, opaqueness, and water absorbancy. Moths might be a problem. Because a felt cover can weigh four times more than a canvas covering, a solid wooden frame is mandatory. Even two or three layers of felt are so thick that, except for the door and the *tono*, little or no light passes through, making for a very dark *ger*.

FELT

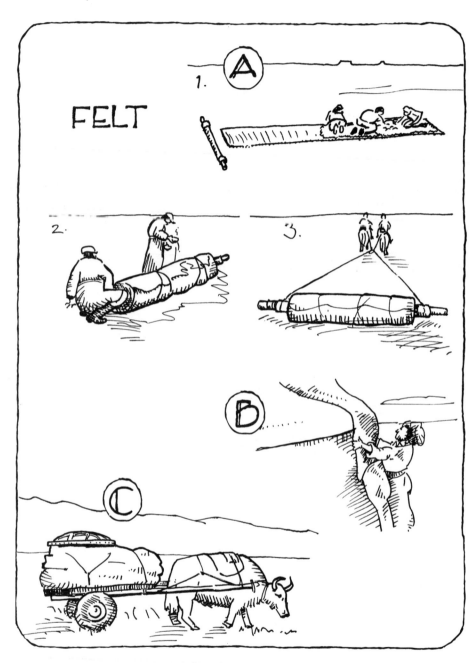

Felt Making

The felt-making process: A reed mat or "mother" felt, slightly larger than the desired piece of felt, is laid out flat, and covered with 3 to 5 inches of fluffed wool in thin layers *(A1)*. To make a design, colored bits of wool or cloth are arranged on the mat before the bulk is laid out.

The mat is then carefully rolled around a heavy wooden axle, wetted until sodden, and tightly bound with skins, cloth, and ropes *(A2)*. The bundle is rolled for hours across the plain *(A3)*. The wool fibers begin to rub against each other, creating heat, which causes the fibers to kink up, resulting in felt. The mat is rolled out again, and any weak areas are retouched with more wool. After re-rolling, the felt is peeled off and laid out to dry.

In the coldest months of winter, as many as eight layers of felt will cover a *ger*, with a final cover of canvas or other material.

Other Cover Details

This woman is adding a final, one-piece canvas cover over many layers of felt *(B)*. In most cases, it seems the weight of the frame and felt is enough to stabilize the *ger* in the wind. The form-fitting, custom cover is held in place by three ropes that wrap around the wall and attach to the *nars,* the door frame below it. The roof skin is held in place by a rope binding *(p. 8, B)*, a network of cables on the outside of the *ger*, tied to heavy stones. It not only holds the cover on firmly, it further stabilizes the whole structure.

This yak is pulling a cart that carries the *tono* and cover for a *ger.* Another cart the same size bears the rest of the frame *(C)*.

KEEPING COOL

COOKING WITH DUNG

Fresh Air!

For circulation, the cover can be lifted on the windward side *(A, opposite)*.

The Open Fire

An open fire can look and feel great, but it also requires your constant attention while it's burning, to keep the *ger* free of smoke and fumes. The ancient *ger* had a central wood- or dung cake–burning brasier *(C, opposite)*, and the shape of the *ger* had an extra curve at the top to more easily guide the smoke out. *(See* Genghis Khan's *ger,* "The Drawings of Donn P. Crane," *p. 125).*

Even so, as soon as metal stoves became available, they were standard in all *ger*s.

Dung Cakes

The fibrous dry manure of camels, horses and other livestock *(B)* easily converts into handy fuel-discs when shaped and dried in the sun, for burning in specially designed braziers. Camel dung burns with a low, long-lasting and virtually smoke-free flame.

Dung brasiers have largely fallen out of use since the arrival of the smoke-free wood/dung–burning stove. Consequently, you won't see a *ger* without a stovepipe very often, but dung cakes are still sold in the markets.

Dung Braziers

Collected dry livestock dung is placed in a shallow pit, and water is added until "patties" are easily formed. These dung cakes are dried in the sun, and stored for use in an open brazier *(C)* or a modern stove with a chimney. Ventilation is essential when using a brazier indoors, so that smoke and fumes can escape.

A fancier, better-preserved brazier on display in a Mongolian museum exhibit

BONES

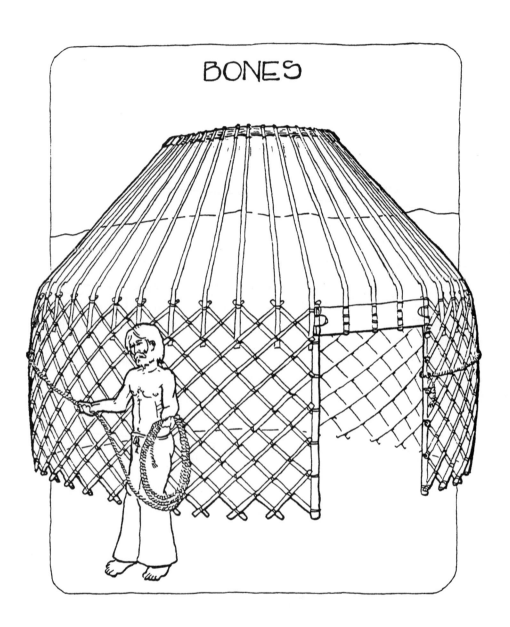

2
BONES I

The "bones" are the pole framework of the yurt. On the opposite page, with the cover removed, you can see the Johnson grass frame and willow smokehole ring as described in this chapter. You'll find some alternate frame-building ideas in "Bones II," at the end of this chapter.

Roots

The most difficult aspect of developing this yurt was designing the frame. I wanted it to be organic *and* easy to erect; true to the Mongolian ideal, but geared to the climate and materials surrounding me. I was also broke. Any extra money had to go into the canvas cover. My plan was to re-use cast-off materials wherever natural materials wouldn't work.

I built my first yurts entirely out of willow poles, which were readily available but impossibly crooked. I've since learned that in Mongolia and Europe, willow, poplar, ash, hazel, and other woods are specially chosen varieties, cultivated to grow extremely straight *(see p. 18)*. Let me just say that my first attempts were *very* organic, but nightmarish to assemble.

I also tried wood lath from the lumberyard, but I was dissatisfied with its square feeling in an otherwise round space, not to mention the prohibitive cost of the high-quality wood required. (To bend evenly, they must have no knots.) Visiting Santa Cruz, California, I discovered Johnson grass, an invasive relative of sugar cane, and my search was over.

What You'll Need – "Bones"

Materials
- About 150 poles, 10' to 15' long
- 4 car tire inner tubes (used)
- Willow (about 35 young shoots)
- Wood (6" lath, 41" long)
- Two stout poles (7' long)

Tools
- Pruning saw
- Tape measure
- Scissors

The car tire inner tubes called for in the list above are for cutting into strips to make rubber bands. This is what I used in my early yurts, but I discovered that rubber in the sun and elements begins to break down after two or three years. I now recommend nylon cord.

In the tool department, you'll need a small pruning saw for harvesting poles and a saw with finer teeth for making the final cuts, as well as a tape measure and a hefty pair of scissors. The frame design I offer here is a conglomeration of a number of yurts seen in old photos and drawings. I especially like the way the wall curves up into the roof ("Kazakh"-style), as opposed to a sharp angle ("Mongolian"-style), and generally the smoother lines resulting from the large number of poles.

TALL, SKINNY PLANTS

Tall, Skinny Plants

Here are three possibilities for frame material. If you intend to cut your own poles from the forest, spend some time looking around in your own neck of the woods for trees and shrubs that naturally have a straight, vertical nature. Collect some samples and let them dry.

The illustration at left shows the basic differences between bamboo (leafy at the top) and Johnson grass (plume at the top). Although the guy in the drawing is cutting Johnson grass, in real life he'd go for the bamboo growing three feet away. This also shows what willow, used for the smokehole ring and cover, looks like.

Bamboo

The over 1400 species of bamboo are members of the grass family *(Gramineae)*. They grow from rhizomes (underground plant stems). Some species are hardy down to −10°F, but often bamboo in colder climates won't grow tall enough or vigorously enough to be useful for yurt construction.

Bamboo is generally divided into two broad categories—running and clumping. Running varieties have given the clumping varieties a bad name. Clumpers don't have the annoying habit of suddenly popping up in the middle of your lawn, or your neighbor's lawn. All bamboos mentioned in this book are of the clumping kind.

Although only two species of bamboo are native to North America (*Arundinaria macrosperma* and *A. tecta*), several Asian species have been successfully transplanted to locations near the U.S. coast, including areas by the Gulf of Mexico. Today, actual small forests of bamboo can be found in these areas. With proper mulching, some kinds of bamboo can be grown in quite cool climates.

Johnson Grass

The leaves on Johnson grass, *Sorghum halepense (B)*, as opposed to bamboo leaves, grow upward directly off each joint like a cornstalk. Its seeds are contained in a tuft at the top. Like bamboo, Johnson grass is a member of the grass family, *Gramineae*. It is considered a pest and you should have no trouble getting permission to cut it; just be sure you're not transporting invasive grass seeds with your poles.

The yurt I lived in, in the late 70's (the one described in these plans), is made from Johnson grass cut in a backyard in Santa Cruz, CA, for free, and transported to New Mexico. I've gotten this same species (again for free) behind a gas station in Albuquerque, NM. I should mention though, that because of the considerably cooler winters in New Mexico, second-year poles were rare and I barely got enough for one yurt from a stand of thousands.

I've learned the hard way that the quality of the final structure can only be as good as the quality of the raw materials, so choose your poles carefully.

Other kinds of hollow grass, cane or reed growing to a similar height (12 to 20 feet) and thickness (1 to 1½ inches at the base) can also be used for hollow pole yurts.

Willow

Many varieties of willow, *Salix purpurea (C)*, grow around North American lakes, and alongside rivers, streams and irrigation ditches. The drawing gives you a general idea of the buds, leaves, and stature of this useful plant. It can be cultivated to grow straight and without branches.

Coppicing

Coppicing is the ancient practice of cutting a "mother" tree to the ground in order to force the growth of many fast-growing "suckers." There were many uses in history for the resulting 1″–3″ sticks, besides firewood of a convenient size. Before barbed wire, these tall, skinny poles were harvested and woven between fenceposts to contain livestock. The sticks are also used for wattle-and-daub building as well as the supporting frame under thatched roofs. *(See illustration, p. 140.)*

Hazel (*Coryllus avellana*), as well as ash, poplar and willow, has been grown in this way in Europe for generations. Although there's less call for the harvested wood these days, craftspeople, and now yurt builders, are creating a market for the poles.

Cutting Poles

All of these tall, skinny plants grow naturally in crowded stands, and periodic pruning will increase the remaining plants' vitality. Cut them as close to the ground as possible, for the health of the roots and the appearance of the stand. Learn to recognize first-year, second-year, and older plants, as the second-year ones are best. They've completed their upward growth, but are still strong and bendable.

Gathering the Poles

Collect 150 good straight poles, 1 to 1½ inches in diameter at the base and tapering to no less than the size of your pointing finger after 8 feet. Cut them as close to the ground as possible and clean them of branches, carefully working *up* the plants so as not to weaken them at the limb connections.

The stand of whatever you're cutting will grow stronger with thinning, so say a prayer and cut the poles you need. Cut two poles to be the sides of your door, about 2 inches in diameter and 7 feet long.

Cutting the Rafters

Select 45 of the stoutest, straightest poles and saw them to 7 feet, cutting the top end of each at a "knuckle," about an inch in diameter. These are the rafter poles.

Cutting the Tubes

Each rafter pole connects to the smokehole ring by means of a 6-inch tube cut from a slightly thicker cane *(right)*. These tubes are custom fit so that each rafter is mated to a particular tube. Rafters and tubes are labeled so that all poles have a tight fit. When the smokehole ring is finished, these tubes will be tied to it using inner tube rubber bands.

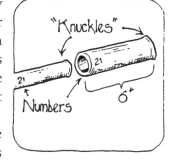

Put all the rafter poles in one place, all oriented the same way. You'll be working with the top, skinny ends of the poles.

Make 6-inch tubes to fit onto the top of each rafter. Find a fat cane and cut a 6-inch section, with a knuckle at one end and open at the other. By trial-and-error, find a rafter pole tip that fits this tube firmly and leave it there. Match all rafter ends in this way so that you have 45 rafters, each fitted with a tube. When you're finished, store the rafters out of the sun.

Seasoning and Bending the Latticework Poles

When the yurt is complete, the *khana*, the latticework wall sections, are at a 45°

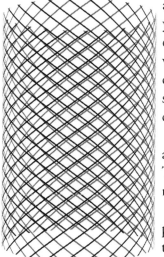

angle and must curve around the circular wall if the yurt is to have straight sides. Using this yurt as an example of yurt wall geometry, the poles of the lattice wall are defining a 5-foot high section of an invisible cylinder, 13 feet in diameter, in two sets of 45° parallel spirals each, twisting in opposite directions around the cylinder wall.

If the poles are left straight, the yurt wall will have an inward curve in the middle, like a narrow waistline. This effect can be lessened by putting the poles at a more vertical angle.

Yurt builders in Mongolia will sometimes leave the poles straight, but it's more common to put a curve in the top end of the wall poles. This makes a wall slightly wider at the bottom, increasing stability in high winds.

PREPARING THE POLES

A The lattice poles

LENGTH IN MARKS

NUMBER NEEDED

8" 2"

16   16   16   16   64

C The rafters

CUT   "KNUCKLE"

20"   7'

1.

2.

3.

B Pole-bending

1.

2.

3.

The extra curve at the top of the wall also makes a smoother, more aerodynamic transition from wall to roof. In this yurt, I bent my poles along their entire length using direct heat.

Cutting the Poles for the Latticework

Cut 64 of the remaining poles to 8 feet 4 inches. These are the longest poles in the latticework wall. This will result in a wall about 6 feet high. For a chart of other wall heights and yurt sizes, see p. 100.

Pick a pole to be used as a measuring stick for the others. Make a mark 2 inches from the base with a permanent marker, and another mark every 8 inches, until you have thirteen marks—that is, twelve 8-inch sections with 2 inches left over at either end. Use this pole to mark the other 63. These marks are your guides to be used in tying later on.

You'll also need some shorter poles, which you can measure, cut and mark using your measuring pole and the chart opposite *(A)*. It tells you the length in marks (always leave 2 inches at either end of each pole) and the number needed of each size.

In choosing the latticework poles, you'll have to put a slight curve in all of them, so be aware of the natural curve of the poles and use it to your advantage.

To bend the poles with direct heat *(B)*, you'll need a hot fire and a stream or a big basin of cold water. Draw a 9-foot section of a circle with an 8-foot radius on the ground as a guide for bending the first pole.

Heat a 3-foot section at a time (leave cool places for your hands), turning the pole constantly so that it doesn't burn *(B-1)*. Then, using your thumbs as levers, gently bend the pole *(B-2)* and immerse it in the water *(B-3)*. This will temper the bend. Then do another 3-foot section. As you go, compare the curve with the one you drew on the ground, copying it as best you can. Once you have one pole right, use it as a standard for the others.

By the way, one of the great pleasures of building this yurt is the aroma of roasting Johnson grass, similar to roasted corn.

Bending the Rafters

Because the rafters are thicker than the latticework poles and require a more extreme bend, you'll have to flatten part of the bottom end of each pole before bending it *(C)*. To do this, first cut a notch 20 inches from the base end, about a third of the way (no more!) through the pole at an angle as shown in *(C-1)*. Prepare all 45 rafter poles this way.

Then, just below the notch, heat the pole over a fire *(C-2)*, and, flattening a 10-inch section below the notch with your foot (wear shoes!), bend the pole to about a 45°

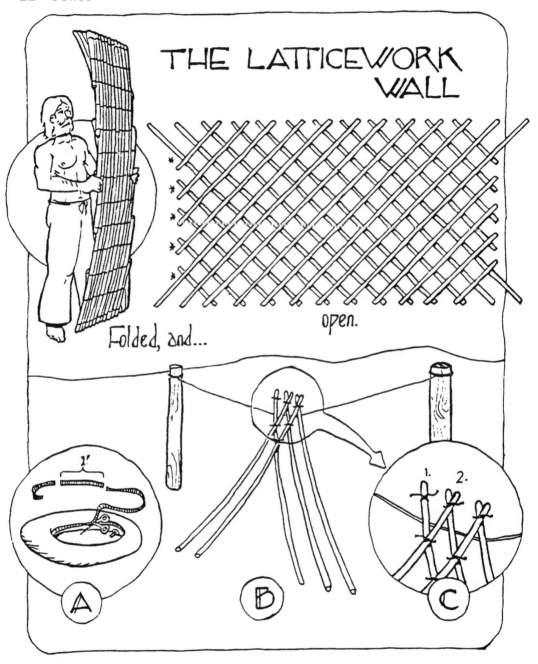

THE LATTICEWORK WALL

Folded, and...

open.

A

B

C

angle, by gently lifting the long end, curving the flattened section evenly *(C-3)*. Heat the bend again and cool it in cold water as you did the latticework poles.

Do one pole and make it the standard for the others. When you're finished, set the poles aside.

To insure against splitting, wrap tape around the openings in the tubes and around the rafters, just above the notch. I used all-weather electrical tape.

The Latticework Wall

Each section of the latticework wall, or *khana (opposite),* is made in four sections, each of which accordions in and out like a baby gate. At top left, a section of wall is shown folded up, and at top right, it's shown opened.

Rubber Bands

For tying the wall together, you'll need about 700 rubber bands which you will cut from used car inner tubes. Start on the inside of the tire tube next to the nipple and spiral away from it, making a long half-inch-wide strip *(A, opposite)*. Cut this strip into 12-inch lengths. You should be able to get all the rubber bands you need from four or five tubes; ask at gas stations or tire dealers.

Although the inner tube rubber bands work well, they degrade in the elements over time. You can also use 15-inch lengths of heavy cord. Use the same knot system recommended below. See "Bones II," at the end of this chapter, for a drilling and tying system using nylon cord.

Tying

For ease in tying the latticework sections, a rope strung between two trees or posts about 12 feet apart at a height of about 4½ feet is helpful *(B)*.

Divide the marked and curved poles into four groups, each with sixteen long ones and four of each smaller size. Begin by tying two full-length poles together at the top mark. Wrapping the rubber band behind the pole, tie a square knot *(C-1)*, then bring the ends around and tie the second pole *(C-2)*. Make sure all the knots are on the *inside* of the bend in the pole. If you're leaning your work on a rope as mentioned above, the poles will naturally keep the bend down and the knotted side up.

Important: As you begin each section, see that the poles slant from *left to right* going up the wall. This is essential in fitting the wall sections together. Using the wall section shown at top right on p. 22, as a guide, first add a pole on top, then one underneath. Save the shorter poles for last. Note that the five intersections (marked with asterisks) are left untied.

When you're finished with all four wall sections, lay two of them out, knotted side up, and on one cut the two longer corner poles at the top and bottom right-hand side flush with the other poles along the edge. Do the same on the other section, only this time cut the top and bottom *left-hand* corner poles and tie all the junctions between. These will be the door sections.

The Door Frame

See pp. 42–43 for other ways to make a door frame. This door frame is made of two *posts (A)* and a wooden *lintel (B),* which is notched for easy tying to both the posts and the rafters *(C).*

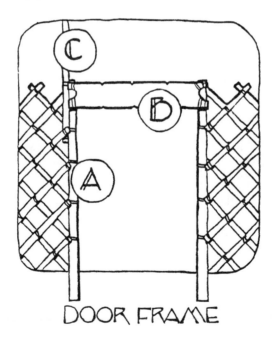

DOOR FRAME

Door Posts

The door posts should be 7 feet long and of thicker wood than the frame (not necessarily hollow), about 2 inches thick at the base, narrowing to not less than an inch at the top. They should be smooth and straight.

Since these posts will be set into the ground one foot, use redwood or cedar, or soak their bottom ends in motor oil or some other sealer.

The Lintel

To make the door lintel, you'll need a 41-inch length of 6-inch lath, cut as you see here. It's notched so that it can be tied into the frame.

A curve in the door lintel to match the curve of the wall will avoid unsightly bumps in the lines of the tent. To make this curve, soak the lintel under water for three or four days (after it's been cut and notched), then set it like a bridge between two logs or blocks and weight the center down with stones until it gets the right curve.

To measure this curve, lay a straightedge from one end of the lintel to the other. At the center of the straightedge, the lintel should be bent 2 inches below it. Leave the rocks on until the wood is completely dry.

THE SMOKEHOLE RING

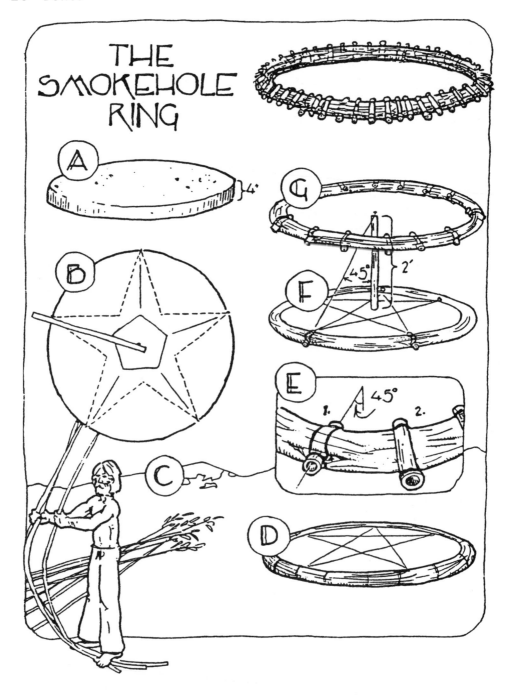

The Smokehole Ring

The smokehole ring consists of a 4-foot diameter ring of woven willow or other bendable green sticks. Forty-five hollow tubes are fastened to it by means of inner tube rubber bands. These will receive the rafter poles.

The Form

Before you begin weaving the ring, make or find a rigid form so that you get an accurate circle. A tight ring of stakes driven into the ground, a big metal tub, or wheel rim might work. A round mud platform 4 feet in diameter and 4 inches thick is an excellent form *(A, next page)* and, if you make it on your future yurt site, it can be your fireplace platform, too. *(See "Luxury Extras," p. 78.)*

A five-pointed star scratched on the still-soft surface of the platform will be useful in locating the first five rafters in the ring *(B)*: First make a newspaper pentagon with each angle 108° and each side 18 inches. Wet the surface of the mud platform and push the pattern through a nail in the center of the circle. Then, with a straightedge, sight from the nail through each of the corners of the pentagon, marking five points along the edge of the platform. Remove the paper pentagon and the nail, and join the points with your straightedge to make a star as shown.

On the following page, there is a 45-pointed star pattern. Bring it to a copier or scanner and enlarge the pattern to fit an 8.5 × 11-inch sheet (or larger) sheet of paper. Carefully measure to find the exact center of the platform, and drive a long nail through the paper into the platform. Secure the pattern to the platform with tacks or small nails. The five equally distributed support rafters are **bold**.

The Ring

For the ring itself, cut twenty young green poles of willow or some other similar plant *("Tall, Skinny Plants," p. 17)* about 12 feet in length, with a diameter at the base about the same as your pointing finger. Trim branches off and pre-bend them as you did for the border around the smokehole cover *(Smokehole Ring, opposite)*.

To begin weaving *(C, opposite)*, twist three poles together while pinning their thick ends down with your foot. Add one pole at a time, always working in the same direction, from the base end to the tip, until you've got a curving cord six to eight poles thick and long enough to overlap itself some when laid out along the outside of the form. Work the ends of the cord together to make a ring. Add more poles to reinforce it, always spiraling in the same direction.

The ring should be at least ten poles thick all the way around. When you've got a good circle just big enough to fit tightly onto the form, ease the ring down. It should resist some. Weight it down with rocks and leave it to dry *(D)*. Drying will take one to three weeks, depending on the weather.

Numbers

On the smokehole ring, because of the variation in the ends of the rafter poles, it's going to be necessary to match each rafter pole to a particular tube on the ring. Also, because there's variation in the rafter poles, we'll select out the strongest, the *support rafters*, and space them evenly around the roof frame.

The numbering begins at the left side of the door, if you were standing inside, or hovering over the top of the yurt, with poles 1, 2, and 3 resting on the lintel, and 4 being the first support rafter. The support rafters are highlighted in the diagram.

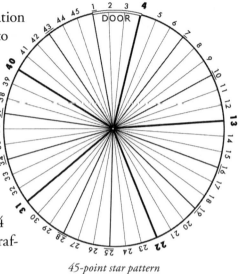

45-point star pattern

The Tubes

While you're waiting, you can number the rafters and the matched tubes that will be part of the smokehole ring. Back when you cut the rafters, you also cut 6-inch tubes for the top ends of each of the poles. *(See "Cutting the Tubes," p. 19.)*

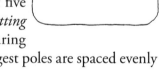

Lay out the rafters with the tubes still on and choose the five stoutest. These will be the support rafters, the first five you'll connect in the final assembly of the yurt *("Putting It All Together," p. 68)*. This gives increased stability during assembly when it's most needed, and ensures your strongest poles are spaced evenly around the roof.

Since the poles and tubes are matched, they must be numbered—on each tube, next to the opening, and on the rafter near the tip, as shown here, using a weatherproof marking pen, like a Sharpie.

The five main support rafters (and tubes) should be numbered 4, 13, 22, 31, and 40. This will space them evenly about the ring.

The ten next stoutest poles are numbered 1, 7, 10, 16, 19, 25, 28, 34, 37, and 43. These will be the second group of poles, again to get the best load distribution.

Number the remaining poles from 2 to 45, skipping the numbers already used.

Rafters numbered 1, 2, and 3 will be the rafters over the door. When the frame is otherwise assembled, these will be custom-cut.

Tying Tubes to Ring

When the woven ring is fairly dry, take all the numbered tubes off the rafters and bring them to the ring along with fifty rubber bands. (*See p. 23* for inner tube cutting instructions.) Remove the ring from the form and carefully saw off any ends that can't be tucked in.

A peg, driven firmly into the center of the mud platform so that it stands 2 feet high, with a string about 3 feet long tacked to the top of it, will be your angle guide as you install the tubes. This can be seen on p. 26.

From the tubes, select the five that will house the support rafters (numbered 4, 13, 22, 31, and 40, *opposite*). Beginning with the tube labeled 4, work it through the woven ring (*E-1, p. 26*), using the string guide to get as close to a 45° angle as possible. The open end should be pointing down and out from the ring (*F*). A small crowbar or a large screwdriver is helpful in opening places in the ring for the tubes.

The fit won't be exact, but get it as close as you can. To ease the pressure on the tubes, 3-inch lengths of solid wood can be inserted on either side of the tube, if it seems necessary. When it's right, secure the tube with rubber band loops both over and under the ring as shown.

Place the ring back on the form with this first tube at one of the points of the star. Tube number 13 goes exactly at the next point, moving clockwise around the ring, 22 after that and so on until you have all five angled accurately, spaced evenly, and securely attached (*F, p. 26*). Take time to do these well, for the stability of the yurt will depend on them.

Then set ten more tubes into the ring in the same way, two between each of the first five (*G*). You can carefully eyeball the spacing here, although the angle must be fairly exact.

The remainder of the tubes are tied *over* the ring (*E-2, p. 26*). Make another circuit, adding the rest of the tubes, that is, two more between each two already on the ring.

A well-made smokehole ring is a work of art.

BONES II – Other Ways

Now we'll talk about some alternative ways of constructing the frame. This part of the book is all new, and although I built the yurt illustrated here from bamboo, all the techniques described here apply to solid-pole yurts as well, with the exception of the *nars*, the door frame.

Since the original *Mongolian Cloud Houses* was written, 25 years ago (yikes!), a lot has happened.

Maui life and Maui's climate were completely different. To get back into the spirit for the new book, it seemed necessary to build another yurt.

My gardening clients, Maui Animal Rescue and Sanctuary (MARS), said they'd like a bamboo-framed yurt to use as a walk-in birdcage—an aviary! Their idea was to suspend ultralight metal aviary netting from the inside of the frame. This is one yurt use I wouldn't have expected, but it sounded cool! . . . and it would be made of the local bamboo.

I began looking for bamboo to cut, pulling my resources together on bending and seasoning, looking for low-tech, low-cost solutions to each challenge.

The bamboo yurt frame is now complete. We await the netting. Three months after my departure from Maui, the frame still stands, but aviary cloth intended to be hung from the inside has not appeared. I'm concerned for the bamboo, exposed as it is to damp weather, uncovered.

Following are some new tricks and suggestions for adapting the basic yurt design.

All these years later, looking back at my ideas, using light, hollow poles connected with recycled inner tube rubber bands, I wonder if I'd do it *that* way again.

The advantages of tying the frame together with inner tube rubber bands—the materials are free, there's no drilling of poles, the frame has a lot of "give," allowing for irregular poles—fail to outweigh the impermanence of rubber in the sun and weather. After two seasons, the rubber bands would crack and break where they touched the canvas. Solution: rubber conditioner? Some other tying material? Nylon cord?

The techniques described in this section are appropriate for both solid and hollow poles, with the exception of the door design, made, in this case, of 3-inch bamboo. On p. 100, you'll find specifications for a 13-foot yurt, and other sizes.

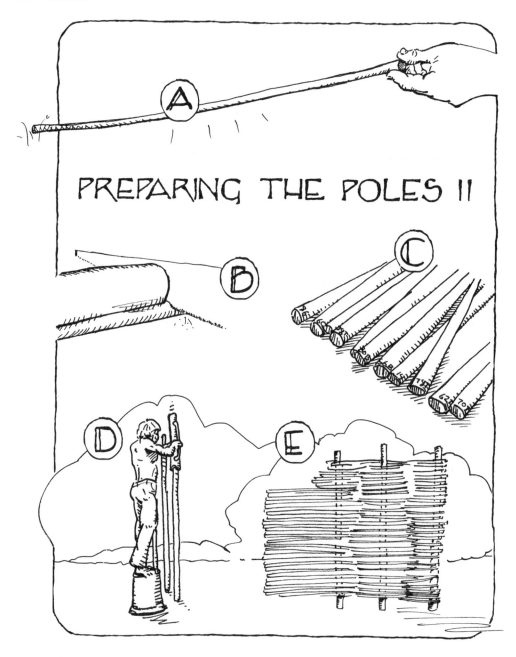

PREPARING THE POLES II

Preparing the Poles II

Final Cut

When making the final cuts for the wall poles, keep them in three groups: rafter poles, full-length wall poles, and one group of all the shorter-length poles.

These should be carefully marked, so you can find each size easily when you're putting the frame together *(C)*.

When cutting multiple poles of the same length, you can use one pole to measure the others *(B)*.

Drilling the Poles

There are many ways of putting together a frame. Throughout Central Asia there are many variations on the basic design, but usually the poles are drilled, and secured with leather "hinges."

Before drilling, check to find the natural bow in the pole by gently holding one end and resting the other end on the ground. The holes you drill should be into this curve, not across it.

Another way of putting a curve in your poles is to use a form: the latticework wall poles are woven between the vertical poles *(D & E)*. Each pole is put into the form opposite the pole below. Some poles may fail. That's why you cut extra, yes?

If you like the Kazakh-style, curved roof line, you'll need to bend all your rafter poles near the lower end. The *uni*-bending form described by Paul King in *The Complete Yurt Handbook* works well. *(See p. 128.)*

Handy Jigs

The contraption at *A-1* is for drilling the first hole on each pole. The end of the pole is pushed into the groove up against the stop *(A-2)*. On poles that have one end at the top of the wall, the top hole is 2 inches from the end of the pole and the bottom hole is 4 inches from the end. On poles that have one end at the bottom of the wall, the first hole is 4 inches from both ends *(A-3)*.

The jig shown at *B* is for the rest of the wall pole holes. The nail goes through the first hole *(B-1)*, showing you where to put the next one *(B-2)*. Drill no more than two additional holes at each end of the poles *(B-3)*. The middle area of the wall is left untied, to allow for irregularities in the poles.

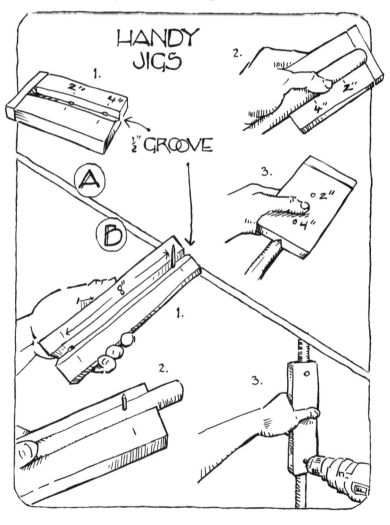

HANDY JIGS

1.

2.

½" GROOVE

A

B

3.

1.

2.

3.

Khana — **Latticework Wall II**

Millions of knots! Well, not millions, but a lot.

Drilling holes and tying knots is a lot of work, but you can make the work easier and faster with a little planning. First, cut a length of nylon cord about 4 feet long and tie a knot at one end.

At the other end of the nylon cord, you can heat about 2 inches to where the cord begins to melt *(A)*. Carefully rub the ***very hot*** end of the string between your fingers (use gloves) until you have a hardened end that will easily push through the holes.

I usually start at the top and center of a wall section, choosing two full-length poles. After carefully determining which one goes on top (the one rising from the bottom left to right) ***and*** making sure they both curve the same way. For more help getting started, see "The Latticework Wall," p. 22, *B & C*.

Push the hardened end of the nylon cord up through the bottom pole, then up through the upper pole *(B)*. Pull the string through until the knot catches *(C)*. Tighten the cord, cut close to the knot, tie a knot, and burn the end, smashing down the molten nylon with your calloused finger, if you can stand it.

LOTS OF KNOTS

THE SMOKEHOLE RING II

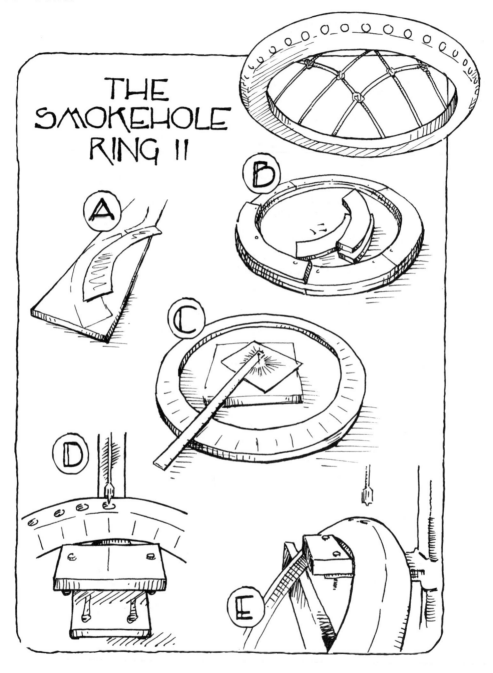

Tono — Smokehole Ring II

You can make a solid wood smokehole ring out of store-bought lumber. This 35-foot *tono* used four 1″ × 10″ × 6′ fir planks from Home Depot (forgive me!). The curves were cut with a jigsaw, the flat ends with a circular saw.

The patterns for this ring are on p. 102. Make twelve of the quarter-circles. Make sure the ends are square and flat. You'll have to lay out the pieces on the floor and move them around for a good fit.

Be sure to overlap the joint *(B)*. Glue and screw, keeping the screws near the inside of the ring, because you'll be drilling 3-inch holes in from the outside edge of the ring. Clamp and let dry overnight. Smooth the ring and sand.

Mark the holes for the rafter poles using the appropriate pattern from p. 102. Stabilize the ring and position the pattern in the exact center of the circle, raised up so it's the same level as the top face of the ring. Make sure everything is secure, then carefully tap a small nail into the center of the pattern.

Rest a straightedge against the nail and adjust until one of the lines on the pattern is exactly parallel to the straightedge *(C)*. Draw a line lightly in pencil across the top face of the ring. Continue around the ring, line by line.

Smokehole Ring Holes

A drill press is the ideal tool for quickly and accurately making the 1-inch holes around the outside edge of the *tono*. Bolt a short 2″ × 4″ block onto the drill's shelf to keep the ring from sliding toward you, then solidly brace the lower part of the ring, pulling it out until the correct angle is achieved *(D & E)*.

Set the drill to go about 3 inches into the ring, starting just above the lower outside edge. If you've been careful in your setup, the actual drilling will go fast. Sand the ring in preparation for sealing, coming soon. But first, the smokehole dome.

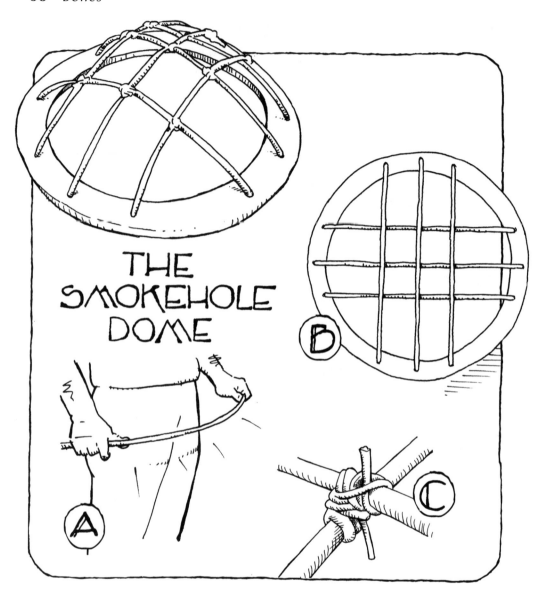

THE SMOKEHOLE DOME

A

B

C

Tono Dome

Now you can add the stick dome that will support a removable smokehole cover. Notice that the holes you'll drill for the sticks must be angled correctly to create two sets of three parallel sticks, perpendicular to each other and rising at about the same angle as the roof *(B)*.

The sticks for the *tono* dome should be no more than about a half-inch in diameter. The holes for the dome should match the diameter of your sticks as closely as possible, so you may need more than one drill bit. Mark all the holes first, and drill carefully, conscious of the correct angles.

Use green sticks and take some time to soften the wood, working a consistent arc into the stick *(A)*. The thicker end will want to stay straight. As you place the sticks, you'll be making many fine adjustments to get a smooth dome.

Tie each intersection with nylon cord, cut short and melt the ends *(C)*.

When all wood is thoroughly dry, apply weather seal to the entire ring.

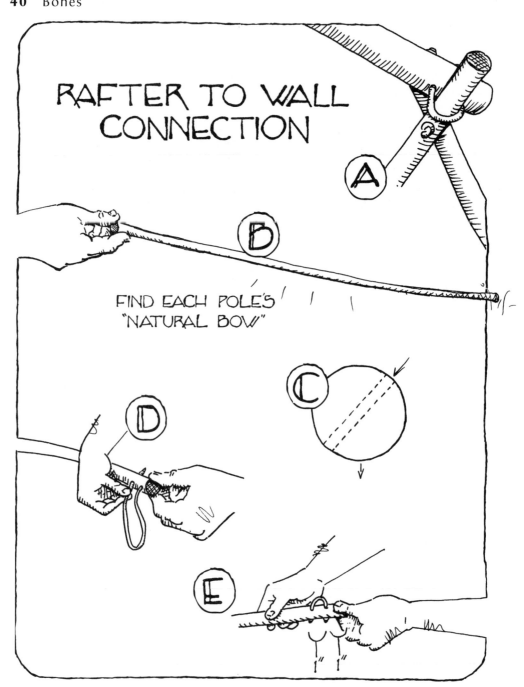

RAFTER TO WALL CONNECTION

FIND EACH POLE'S "NATURAL BOW"

Uni — **Rafters II**

They call this Mongolian-style, as opposed to Kazakh-style, which has the more rounded transition from wall to roof, like those described in "Bones I."

Once again, use the curve of the pole to your advantage *(B)*. The goal is to have any natural bow in each pole curve outwardly. The weight of the canvas will bring the shape into line.

Notice how the rafter sits in the top "X" of the lattice wall *(A)*. The loop is about 45° up from straight down. So, you need to drill two ⅛-inch holes at the bottom end of each rafter pole, 1 inch and 2 inches from the end *(opposite, E)*.

Find the correct angle *(C)* and mark your first pole. The circle is the butt end of a pole; the top end is resting on the ground in front of you. The downward arrow is the curve of the pole; the arrow at the top marks the angle to put two dots, where you'll be drilling. Mark them all, then drill them all.

Use nylon cord, burning the knots *(D)*. Make sure you've got your loop on the correct side when you begin tying.

BAMBOO
DOOR FRAME

Nars – **Door Frame II**

This yurt door was built of four pieces of dry green-stripe bamboo, with hidden plugs, using standard bamboo joinery. I used a borrowed cordless drill.

The horizontals, top and bottom, are 4 feet long, the uprights 5 feet long. A 3-inch-long bamboo plug is chosen to fit tightly ***inside*** each of the uprights. Mark each plug and hole carefully, as diameters will vary.

Measure 6 inches in from the ends of the horizontals *(A)* and make a tight hole for one of the plugs. I used a hole saw for the initial cut *(B)*, and a file bit to shape the hole to the plug *(D)*.

Test the fit as you widen the hole. Pound the plug in with a rubber mallet *(C)*. Make sure the hole at the other end of the horizontal is exactly parallel to this one. The ends of the uprights need to be scalloped to match the curve of the horizontals.

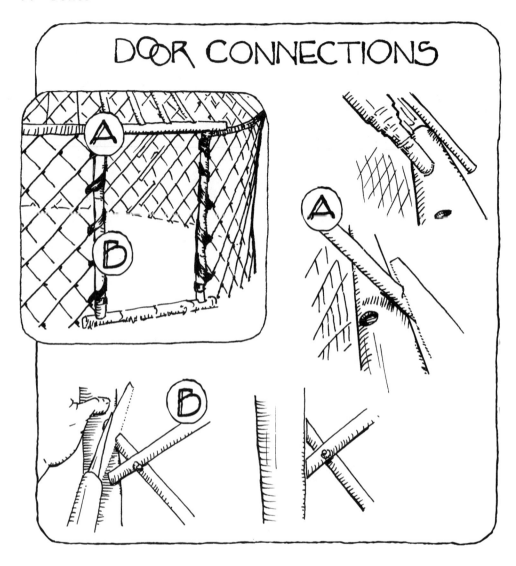

DOOR CONNECTIONS

Rafters to Door Frame

Depending on the frequency of wall poles in your *khana*, the top horizontal of the *nars* will have either three or four rafter poles set into it. Use a drill to make notches for the pole ends. The pole ends will need to be custom-cut to fit.

Wall to Door Frame

The final adjustments for the *nars* are best done when the frame is ready to assemble. Strap the *khana* sections together and set up the wall, as close to the final diameter and wall height as you can. You'll need someone to hold the *nars* as you make vertical cuts *(B)* where the wall meets the door frame. Leave about 1½ inches of pole after the knot.

SKIN

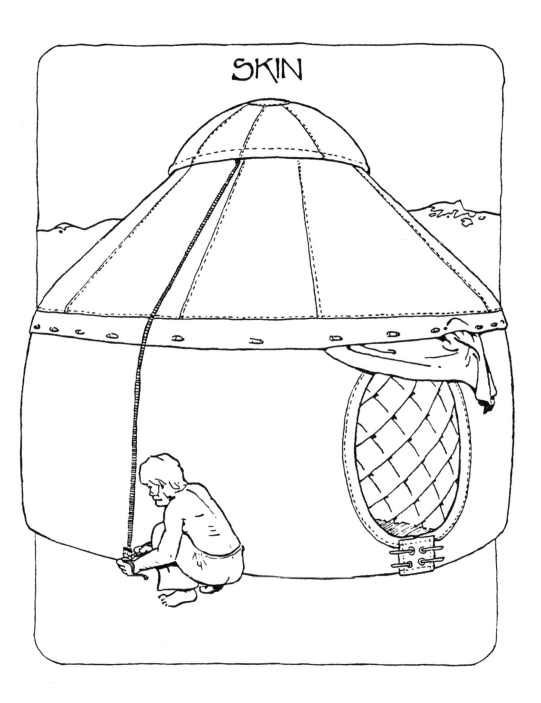

3
SKIN

The first yurt I ever experienced, back in 1977, was wondrous, built by a guy who called himself Sassafras. I was so taken by the quality of the space that I abandoned previous plans to make a tipi my home.

Nestled in the sagebrushed foothills of the Sangre de Cristos Mountains in New Mexico, near a clear reservoir, this was a fairly high-tech yurt—pine lath joined with wing nuts, and an aluminum-conduit-framed smokehole covered with a flat circle of plexiglas. The skin was nylon-reinforced vinyl.

The yurt I describe here is covered with canvas. I broke down and treated mine with a water sealant, and had to let it air out for a few days before moving back in. See p. 94 for other roof cover patterns.

You can sew your own "skin," either by hand as I did on my first yurt (it's meditation!) or by machine. I used 12-ounce untreated canvas. It's strong and natural, but only practical in the driest climates; there are other, un-natural but more durable cover options listed on p. 59. I'll talk about waterproofing at the end of this chapter.

A triangle-pointed needle for hand-sewing canvas is available in most stores with a sewing department, usually coming in a set with four or five other special-purpose needles. For thread get either the waxed nylon kind (from a leather or shoe repair shop) or heavy cotton crochet cord which you can strengthen by rubbing with beeswax. For *machine sewing*, depending on whether you're using a standard or industrial-duty machine, a number 16 or 18 needle is appropriate. Sew with a strong number 16 Dacron thread.

You'll also need a pair of sturdy sharp scissors and a grommet set for half-inch holes, which can be obtained at most hardware stores, if you can't borrow one.

What You'll Need for the Skin

Materials
- 33 yards of 6-foot-wide canvas
- Thread: heavy waxed (for hand sewing), or No. 16 Dacron (for machine sewing)
- 12 yards of heavy nylon cord
- 12 yards of light nylon rope

Tools
- Needle: triangle-pointed (for hand sewing), or No. 16 or 18 (for machine sewing)
- Scissors
- ½-inch hole punch
- Tape measure
- 10-foot straightedge
- String, wood block and a tack

WALL SKIN

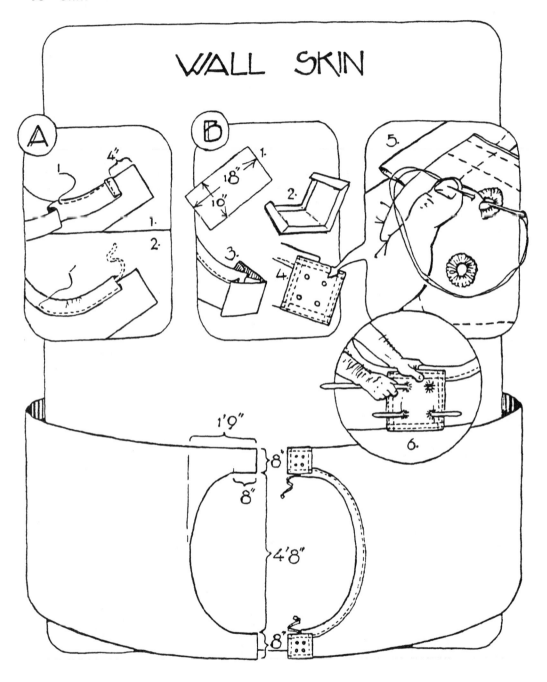

Wall Skin

Cutting

Carefully measure and cut a 43½-foot length of the 6-foot-wide length of canvas. You'll also need two strips, 6 inches wide and 6 feet long, for the border around the door; and four rectangles, 10 by 18 inches, for the grommet reinforcement patches.

All measurements in these plans include the seams, so don't allow any extra.

To draw the door hole, fold the large piece of canvas in half, bringing the two 6-foot edges together. Using the illustration opposite as a guide, measure 8 inches in from each corner of the 6-foot edge and make a mark with a crayon or pencil. From each of these two marks, draw an 8-inch line at right angles to the edge.

Leaving these lines for a moment, find the center of the 6-foot edge, that is 3 feet from either corner. From this point measure 1 foot 9 inches in and make a mark. This is the width of the door. Continuing from the end of one of your 8-inch lines, draw a curve to the halfway point. Do the same from the other 8-inch line.

You now have half the door drawn on the canvas. Cut it out and use it as a pattern for the other half. You can use the pieces you've cut out to make the grommet patch rectangles.

Sewing

Sew the door border first *(A, opposite)*. Begin by folding over one inch on an end of one of the long strips and sewing it. Four inches from a corner of the doorhole, place this strip flush with the edge, with the sewn end facing up *(A-1)*. Begin sewing around the door, keeping the two edges flush. When you get almost to the other corner of the door, cut the strip to allow for another 1-inch hem, and another 4-inch space between the end of the strip and the door corner.

Now fold this strip up and over, forming a tube that will eventually house a tie rope *(A-2)*. Sew again, through all the layers.

For each of the grommet patches, take one of the 10-by-18-inch rectangles *(B-1)* and fold a 1-inch hem all around it. Then fold it in half *(B-2)*, to make an 8-inch square. Slip this piece over one of the door ends so that the edge of the door is sitting against the backbone of the folded square *(B-3)*. Make sure that the end of the door border sits a little above the grommet patch so that a tie rope can go through the door border.

Make double seams all around the square, starting with the outside seams. If you're sewing by hand, a thick piece of leather is handy for pushing the needle through the many layers of canvas.

Finishing Touches

Once all four of these patches are sewn on, you can mark the grommet holes. Center a 4-inch square on each patch, marking the corners with dots *(B-4)*. With a half-inch punch and a hammer (over a block of wood), punch the four marked holes in each patch. These holes can either be set with brass grommets or hand-sewn *(B-5)*.

Run a 6-foot length of cord through each half of the door border, leaving the ends loose. A safety pin secured to the "snaking" end of the cord will make this easier.

The four lacing pins you'll need to hold the wall skin together should be of hardwood, 12 inches long and three-eighths of an inch thick, rounded at the ends and sanded smooth. These can be made either of straight lengths of your local wood or ⅜-inch doweling.

A very early prototype...

ROOF SKIN

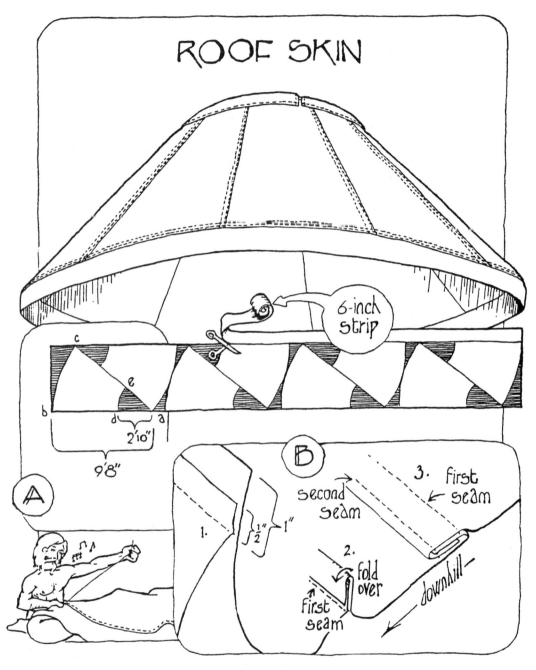

6-inch strip

c

e

b

d   a

2'10"

9'8"

A

B

1.

$\frac{1}{2}$"   1"

3. first seam

second seam

2. fold over

first seam

first seam

downhill

Roof Skin

Cutting

Roll out another 44 feet of canvas and cut a 6-inch strip off the long edge *(opposite)*. If you're careful, you can follow a thread with the scissors. This strip will be the roof overhang—roll it up and set it aside.

The main part of the roof cover is made by sewing eight "pie pieces" into a cone shape. I'll show you how to make the first piece, then you can use it as a pattern for the other seven, staggering them as shown *(A, opposite)* to best use the canvas. Again, let me say that all the patterns here allow for seams.

To make this first piece, you'll need some non-stretching string or wire, a small but fairly heavy chunk of wood (a foot of 2 × 4 will work), a tack and a 10-foot-long straightedge (this can be a piece of lathe, a 2 × 4, or whatever you've got).

Tie a loop at one end of the string, measure 9 feet 8 inches, and make another loop—that's 9 feet 8 inches from loop to loop. Do this again with another piece of string, this time making the length 2 feet 10 inches.

Take the longer string and lay it from the corner of the canvas along the edge from *(B)* to *(A)*, as seen in the illustration. Push the tack through the loop in the string, through the very edge of the canvas at point *(A)*, and into the block of wood. Put a pencil through the loop at the other end of the string and draw the arc from *(B)* to *(C)*.

It helps to have a friend hold the wood block in place, but it's not essential. So *(B)* is the corner and *(C)* is where your marker goes off the canvas. Use your long straightedge to draw a line from *(C)* back to *(A)*.

Now take the long string off the tack and replace it with the short string, leaving the tack where it is. Starting at the edge of the canvas, draw an arc from *(D)* to *(E)*. Cut out this piece and use it as a pattern for the other seven, drawing them all on the canvas first, before cutting, so you get it right.

Besides the eight pie pieces and the roof overhang, cut another three strips, 6 inches wide and 4 feet 3 inches long, for the border around the smokehole.

Sewing

The double-lap "bluejeans" seam I use for sewing the roof skin is both strong and simple *(B, 1, 2 & 3)*, sewn either by hand or machine.

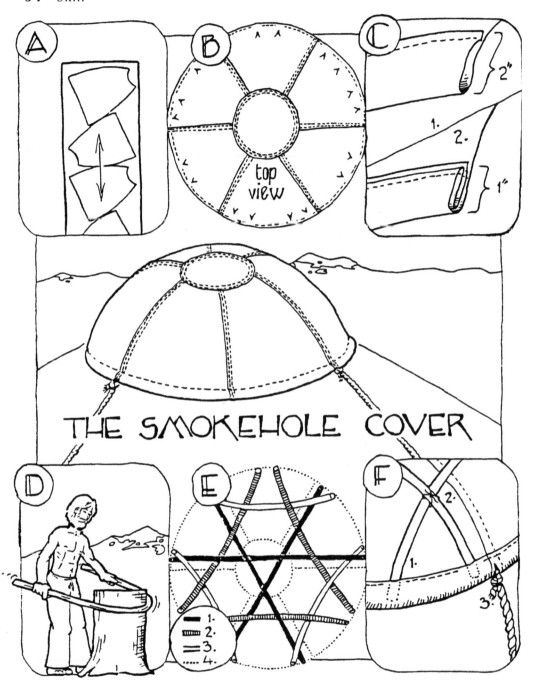

THE SMOKEHOLE COVER

Sew all the pie pieces together first. Then, using the same seam, attach the roof overhang, sewing the cut edge under and making sure that when the seam is folded, the crease is downhill (as in *B-2*), to let water run off.

Sew the smokehole border as you did around the door *("Wall Skin," p. 48, A)*, in three sections with about ¼-inch gap between each strip. A 13-foot length of heavy cord should be worked into this border, the ends tied in a square knot.

The Smokehole Cover

The smokehole cover is a dome sewn like half a beach ball, that is, six rounded triangular sections with a circle at the top. The cover is supported by a willow framework.

The Pattern

You'll find a scaled-down pattern for the smokehole cover skin on the next page. Make a full-size newspaper pattern first, by marking out 1-inch squares on a 2′ 8″ × 3′ sheet of paper and copying the curved lines (once again, seams have been allowed for).

Cutting

Cut the pattern out, and transfer it to the canvas six times, turning the pattern so that the bottom, flat, edge is diagonal to the weave *(A, opposite)*. This will help the canvas stretch to a hemispherical shape.

Also cut a 17-inch circle and mark six equally spaced points around the edge, to be used as sewing guides.

Sewing

Sew the six sections together first, using the double seam *(shown on p. 54, B)*, then add the top circle, matching the six points on the edge with the seams. *Be sure that the lap is downhill*, allowing water to flow over it and not into it.

Fold 2 inches of the cover's border under and sew *(C-1)*, then fold this under and sew once more *(C-2)*, leaving 1-inch gaps in the seam at approximately the locations shown in *(B)*. These gaps are where green sticks will be inserted to reinforce the border and where the framework will be braced inside the cover.

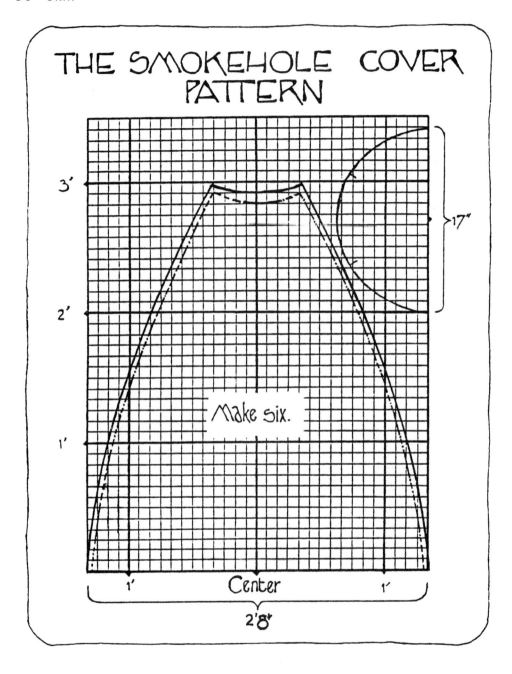

THE SMOKEHOLE COVER PATTERN

Make six.

3'

2'

1'

17"

1'   Center   1'

2'8"

The Framework of the Smokehole Cover

The framework inside the smokehole cover dome is made from young, green, straight sticks — willow, bamboo, Johnson grass, or whatever's available. If you're using solid poles (not hollow), collect fifteen having the thickness of your pointing finger at the base, 8 to 10 feet long. Trim them of branches and put a slight bow in all of them by sliding each along a tree stump or chopping block *(D, p. 54)*.

Take six of the thinnest poles and slip them one at a time into the tube around the base of the cover.

The rest of the framework consists of nine poles, fitted into the cover three at a time *(E-1, 2, & 3)*. (The dotted line, *E-4*, represents the seams on the skin). Begin by cutting your three thickest poles to 6 feet. These will form the center triangle *(E-1)*. Fit them into the underside of the cover, bracing them in the reinforced border at the gaps you left for this reason (this can be seen in *F-1*). Weave them over and under as necessary. You may have to shorten some slightly for a good fit.

The next three poles will be about 5 feet long. Fit them into the cover parallel to and about a foot and a half from the original three *(E-2)*. The last three *(E-3)*, about 4 feet long, go on the opposite sides of the original three.

Be sure the framework is snug against the canvas, then tie all the junctions where the sticks cross with nylon string *(F-2)*.

Ropes

All that remains is to tie the three 12-foot ropes that will secure the smokehole cover *(see p. 54, center)*. At the base of three of the six seams connecting the sections of the cover at the bottom of the reinforced border, make a small slit between the dual seams *(F-3, also p. 54)*.

Slide one end of each rope through a slit in the border, bring it around the stick inside, back out the slit and tie it *(F-3)*. Let the remaining rope hang loose for the time being.

Waterproofing

The roof and wall skin must be treated to resist water. These days there are various high-tech potential cover materials, but canvas still rules. Commercial waterproofing is both expensive and petroleum-based, but it works. Two to three gallons is enough to do my size yurt. In dry climates, you can leave the wall canvas untreated except the bottom foot or so, where ground moisture is a problem. Some yurt makers put a band of waterproof material at the bottom of the wall, extending the life of the skin.

Liquid water seal products can be sprayed on, or can be put on with a brush or roller. To be effective, the canvas must be saturated. The easiest way I've found to apply the waterproofing is with a long-handled roller (the kind used by professional housepainters). With this device you can paint on the waterproofing while the cover is still on the frame, so that as it dries the cover will shrink to a perfect fit. While the cover is still wet, you should go inside and push the rafters up snug against the canvas. *(See illustration, p. 71.)*

The smokehole cover will also stretch some when saturated with waterproofing, but it'll shrink back tight when it dries. For extra protection on the smokehole cover (where rain hits the skin most directly), I've found that a layer of plastic between the frame and the skin makes it impervious to the heaviest downpours. A 6-foot circle of plastic does the trick.

One more thing: after applying commercial waterproofing, be prepared to spend at least one night *not* in the yurt, as the fumes are intense for 36 to 48 hours.

The Painted Yurt

Designs can be added to the cover of the yurt in many ways. Appliqué, stencil, tie-dye, permanent felt-tip markers, and waterproof paint are a few routes you can go. Traditional Mongolian patterns are shown opposite, but since this is a new age, let your imagination go. You might find some inspiration in the patterns found on the Native Americans' medicine tipis.

Nomadic Tipi Makers of Bend, Oregon, have developed what I consider the best fabric for covering a yurt. Here, in their own words, is a description of the material:

All-Weather Canvas

"Over a period of 34 years we have made more than 18,000 tipi covers out of 13 oz. weight Sunforger fabric and we have always offered this as our most durable tipi fabric. The Sunforger treatment was designed to resist the elements of the natural environment. It has limited capacity to withstand the consequences of the man-made environmental corrosiveness of acid rain, chemical air pollutants and intense ultraviolet radiation. Unfortunately, because of the steady increase of these environmental factors, we realize that the 13 oz. canvas with the Sunforger treatment is simply no longer adequate for continued outdoor use. Through these many years we have watched this treatment slowly become less and less effective and in the last five years it is our experience that this 13 oz. weight tipi canvas is only lasting 25% as long as it did 34 years ago.

"As a response to these environmental changes we researched and tested many . . . trade name fabrics such as Pyrotone, Sumbrella, Polaris, Starfire, Suncoat, Polyolifin and Top Gun. For many reasons, none of these commercial industry fabrics met the fabric integrity or long-term performance standards that we were looking for. As a result, we have created our own custom finish that is applied for us to a 100% cotton army duck canvas that itself is woven to our specifications.

"We now offer two extraordinary fabrics that have been treated with a unique All Weather treatment that is 600% denser than the Sunforger treatment. The finished canvas itself is approx. 40% heavier in weight per square yard and it is our expectation that this new fabric will last 3 to 4 times as long as our 13 oz. Sunforger. This unique All Weather treatment is pressure rolled into the canvas fibers and is then heat-set at 350 degrees to ensure the longevity of the fiber integrity. In addition, and of great importance, this weatherization treatment is specially formulated to be highly resistant to ultraviolet radiation. Although it is simply not possible to guarantee that a fabric will be completely mold or mildew proof, the All Weather finish contains the best mold and mildew resistant treatment available today. This canvas will not shrink even 1%, yet the fabric itself retains its breathability."

—Nomadic Tipi Makers, Bend, Oregon
www.tipi.com

THE
YURT KIT

4
PUTTING IT ALL TOGETHER

You did it! You've assembled all the various parts and you're finally ready to erect your own cloud house and move in. But first take inventory to make sure you've got everything, including the *bagana*, the two forked poles you'll need to support the ring while you attach the first rafters.

Then prepare the site. It's up to you how many conveniences you'll have, but even if you're really roughing it, you'll want your spot level and trenched.

With a little experience, the yurt can be erected in less than an hour, though it'll probably take a good deal longer to get things arranged inside just so.

The Yurt Kit

Got everything? The drawing at left shows:

A.	Roof Skin	H.	Door Lintel
B.	Wall Skin	I.	Smokehole Ring, or *tono*
C.	Lacing Pins (4)	J.	Rubber bands (150)
D.	Smokehole Cover	K.	Rope (42′)
E.	Latticework Wall (4 sections, or *khana*)	L.	Door Blanket (6′ × 8′)
F.	Rafter Poles, or *uni* (45)	M.	Safety Pins (25)
G.	Door Posts (2)	N.	Forked Poles, or *bagana* (2)

You'll notice that in addition to the things you've made, the list calls for rope, a door blanket, safety pins, and two forked poles. The rope will only be needed temporarily, until the cover is on the frame. The door is a heavy 6-by-8-foot blanket. The safety pins are the large, nickel-plated kind.

Forked Poles

The forked poles, the *bagana (N, opposite),* are used to support the smokehole ring, or *tono (I),* while attaching the first rafters, and will be removed after all the rafters are in place. It's not unheard-of though, in Mongolian yurts, for decorated *bagana* to remain in place all the time—definitely a good idea where the load from heavy snows are a problem.

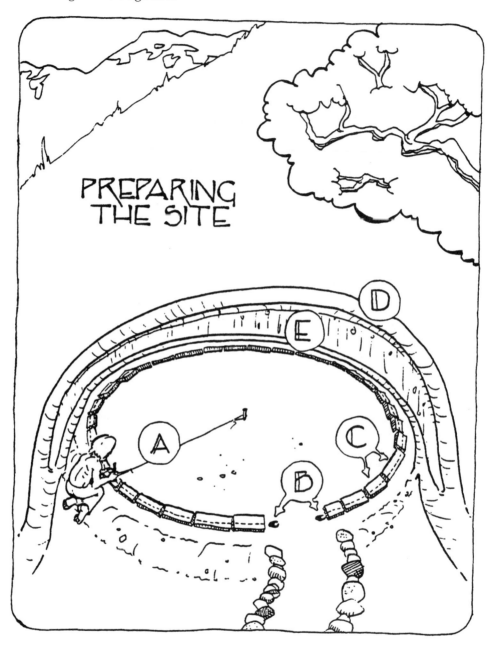

PREPARING
THE SITE

The two long forked poles that hold up the ring in this yurt, are my own simple solution. The two legs of the fork should be about a foot long each, and when standing on the forked end, the poles should rise 9½ feet into the air. If the legs are level at the top, you're assured of a level smokehole ring. Any kind of wood will work, but should be fairly straight.

Preparing the Site

The more level the ground is to begin with, the less work you'll have to do.

Leveling

Use a 6½-foot string looped at either end, as a radius to mark your site *(A, opposite)*, but you should level the ground at least a foot beyond that. Clean the area of any large brush, then move dirt from the uphill side to the lower part.

If you want raised or sunken places, this is the time to make them. It'll be easier to leave dirt on the uphill part than to move it someplace else.

Once the ground is close to level, use a rake to get most of the rocks and pebbles out of the top layer. If water is available, wet the site thoroughly and move dirt to the low places, where water collects. You can use a level and a long 2 × 4 to smooth the surface. This will give you a flat and level floor that can be finished with rugs, stone, wood, or whatever you like.

Post Holes

When the site is level, pound a stake into the center, and draw the circle again *(A, opposite)*. Decide where the door will go, and mark the two door post holes *(B)*. The centers of the holes should be 39 inches apart along the line that indicates the wall. Dig 1-foot-deep holes.

Frame Rest

To keep the bottom part of the frame and canvas from ground moisture, which would eventually rot them, I put a circle of $2'' \times 6''$ mill ends down for the frame to rest on *(C)*. You can get mill ends, which are 2-foot and shorter pieces of planed lumber, at your local sawmill for a few dollars a truckload, but any scrap pieces of uniform width will do. Redwood or cedar, if available, will resist rot.

This frame rest should be slanted down and away from the yurt, for drainage. The circumference of the yurt should be re-marked onto this frame base. Flat rocks, bricks or pavers could also be used.

Trenches

Two trenches on the uphill side of the site are necessary: one to allow water coming downhill to pass around the site *(D, previous page)*, and one for water coming off the yurt itself *(E)*.

The first trench should go above the back wall, uphill from the site. Dig a trench 6 inches deep and a foot wide (bigger if your weather warrants), piling the dirt between the trench and the top of the back wall. Bring the trench around the site until it's below floor level, then angle away from the yurt *(D)*.

The other trench *(E)* goes between the bottom of the back wall and where the yurt will be. Dig it the same as the first, but remove the dirt so that water can flow to the trench easily. Follow the back wall until it can join the upper trench.

Other Preparations

If you want a loft, a refrigerator hole, or a stove platform *("Luxury Extras," p. 82)*, now is the time to install them.

On actual Mongolian *gers*, although there is some variation, the wall-to-wall, *khana*-to-*khana*, connection turns out to be much simpler than what I describe in the next section. **No** overlapping *khana*, **no** numbering of anything.

Above, note the elegant joining of the *khana* sections. It looks like it starts with a loop at the top, the wall sections nesting, but not overlapping, at the tying point.

All holes in the *tono* are the same size, so all *uni*, except the two or three over the door, are interchangeable.

The complex numbering system used here allows for a lot of variability in pole diameter, and assumes you're working with hollow poles.

See "Old Ways," p. 7, and the "Other Sizes," p. 101 as well, for other construction techniques.

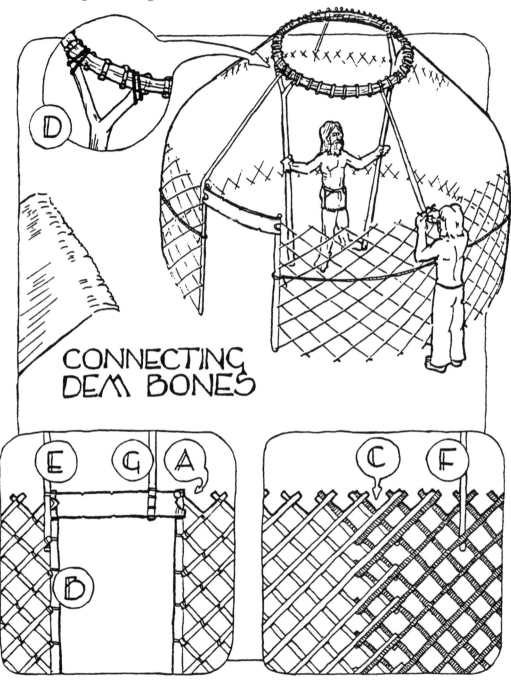

CONNECTING DEM BONES

Connecting the Bones

It'd be handy for you to invite a friend to the yurt erection, particularly at the point of adding the smokehole ring and the first few rafters. Other than that, you can do everything yourself.

On this particular yurt, all connections are tied with the inner tube rubber bands. See "Old Ways," and "Bones II," for other ideas.

The Door Frame

Put up the door first. Set the two *door posts* into the ground so that they stand 6 feet from floor level, and fill in around them with rocks and dirt. Secure the *lintel* to the top of the posts, on the outside, with rubber bands, at each end *(A, opposite)*.

The Latticework Wall

From the latticework wall sections, select the two that you cut specially to go on either side of the door *(see p. 24)*. Expand each of these sections and tie them to their respective door posts *(B, opposite)*. The top corner pole of the wall section should come just to the top of the door post, and the bottom corner should be at floor level, so that the wall is exactly 6 feet high. Tie each place where the wall meets the door with inner tube rubber bands.

To connect the wall sections to one another, first study the drawing *(C)*. Notice how the inside poles of both sections stay on the inside, and note the four points across the top where two parallel poles rest together.

Take one of the remaining wall sections, expand it and slide it into the section tied to the door, keeping the inside poles on the inside. Along the untied edge of the right-hand wall section, the inside and outside poles will spread apart slightly to allow the tied edge of the section on the left to slide through.

When it looks like *(C)*, tie the four places at the top where two poles sit together, then the four corresponding places at the bottom, and finally the untied middle intersections. Tie the other wall-to-wall connections in the same way.

Set the wall frame on the frame rest bordering the floor and adjust it so that it's 6 feet high all around. Tie one end of the 42-foot rope to one of your door posts, about two feet down from the top, and bring it all the way around the outside of the wall. Tie it to the other door post. *(See top right drawing.)* The rope should be a little loose and easy to untie for later adjustments.

Numbers

We have numbers on the tubes around the smokehole ring, and numbers on the rafters. Now we'll number the pole intersections at the top of the wall, to help us get the poles in the right position. The numbers correspond to the numbers on the smokehole ring tubes and the rafters.

Standing at the outside of the door, number the three notched places in the lintel 1, 2, and 3, from right to left, with a permanent marker or crayon. Then number the left door post 4 and continue around the frame, numbering each top "X" until you get back to the right-hand door post, which should be number 45.

The Smokehole Ring and the Rafters

Now is the time to put your friend to work. Get the *smokehole ring,* the two *forked poles,* and the *rafters.* Find the first five support rafters (numbers 4, 13, 22, 31, and 40) and put them where you can get to them easily. The other rafters should be laid out close at hand, in numerical order, with the next ten poles you'll be attaching set forward a bit, so you won't have to fumble around for them later. These are numbers 1, 7, 10, 16, 19, 25, 28, 34, 37, and 43.

Bring the smokehole ring inside the completed wall frame and secure the forked poles to the ring with rubber bands *(D, p. 66).* Carefully raise the ring and, making sure it's level from all angles, turn it so that the numbers

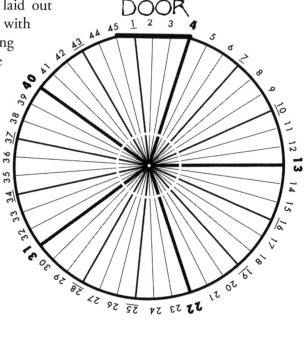

on the ring line up more or less with the numbers marked at the top of the wall. Have your friend continue to support the ring in the center of the floor, while you begin attaching the rafters, the *uni*.

Working on the outside of the frame, do number 4 first, next to the left-hand door post *(E)*. Slide it into the tube numbered 4 on the ring. Note that it goes outside the lintel, then between the poles of the latticework below it. Tie it twice: to the top of the lintel, and, at the bottom of the rafter, to the frame and door post.

Then take rafter number 13, slide it into the proper tube on the ring and tie it to the "X" numbered 13 on the frame. See in the drawing *(F)* how the rafter goes outside the top "X" of the frame, then between the two poles at the intersection below. Tie it twice, at each of those junctions. Attach the other three support rafters in the same way.

You may have to move the frame out a little at this point to match the length of the rafters. Adjust the tension rope so that the wall stands straight up from the floor.

Now, add two more rafters between each of the support rafters. These are the ones you set forward when you laid them out on the ground. Work around the frame, tying them the same as *(F)*, starting with 7 and 10, 16 and 19, and so on. Number 1 is tied to the door lintel with a loop of rubber band *(G)*. By now, your friend's work will be done.

Add the rest of the rafters in one more circuit of the frame, and remove the forked poles. See "Bones II," p. 31, for more ideas and other ways.

Witness the Bones!

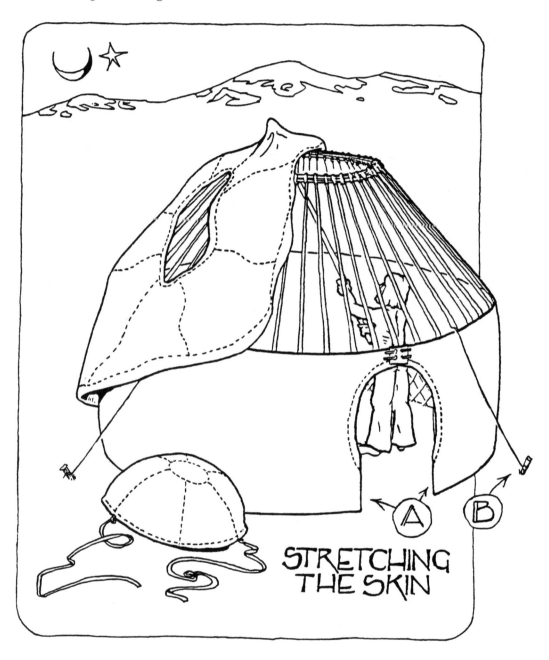

STRETCHING
THE SKIN

Stretching the Skin

Safety pins and lacing pins are an important part of this yurt, safety pins connecting roof and wall, and tipi-like lacing pins joining the ends of the wall skin at the door. (The outer canvas skin on East Asian *gers* is commonly made in one piece, wall and roof pieces sewn together, held tight to the frame with horsehair ropes.)

Wall Skin

Unfold the wall part of the skin and bring it around the frame so that the ends meet at the door. At this stage there is really no top, bottom, inside or outside to it, unless you've specially waterproofed the edge closest to the ground.

Lift the top edge of the wall all the way around, taking out any twists in the canvas, then lift the two top grommet patches and slide a lacing pin in *("Wall Skin," p. 48, B-6)*. You might have to compress the frame, using the tension rope, to do this.

Lift the wall skin up into place on the frame, centering the door on the cover with the door on the frame. The top edge can be temporarily safety-pinned to the rubber bands at the top of the latticework. Slide the rest of the lacing pins into place at the top and bottom of the door.

Roof Skin

Find the outside of the roof skin. This is indicated by the seam holding the roof overhang on, which should allow water to run down over it and not into it. With this side of the roof up, throw an edge of the skin up onto the roof frame so that some of it hangs into the smokehole ring. Then, with a 6-foot pole (safely rounded at the end), you can maneuver the roof skin into place *(as shown opposite)*. Line up the hole on the skin with the smokehole ring on the frame.

Fasten the roof to the wall with safety pins, keeping the roof on the outside and the smokehole centered. Again, there are other ways.

Stretching the Skin

To stretch the skin tightly, push the bottom of each rafter up snugly against the canvas, as shown here. After your first rain, or after waterproofing, the cover will stretch and sag. This is the time to make your skin as tight as a drum. Just push up the bottoms of the rafters and when the canvas dries you'll have a custom fit. (Adjustable rafters are a feature of this rubberized yurt only.)

The Door Blanket

Fold the door blanket in half, to a 4-by-6-foot rectangle. The top edge of the door goes between wall skin and roof skin, where it is pinned around the rafter poles with large safety pins. It should hang just to the ground, no more.

The Smokehole Cover

Throw the smokehole cover up into place, adjusting it with the 6-foot pole from inside the yurt, letting the three ropes dangle to the ground.

At each of the three places where the ropes come to the ground, drive a 2-foot wooden stake into the ground and fasten the rope to it. This will not only hold the smokehole cover on, it'll also secure the yurt in strong winds. Decorate your stakes and tie-downs with stones and colorful flags so you don't stumble over them by accident.

The Summer Door

The door hole on the skin can be folded to the inside at the bottom, where it is tied to the latticework, creating a summer door *(previous page, A)*, allowing readier access and more circulation. You can use mosquito netting if bugs are a problem in the summertime, on the door, and/or over your bed.

Some Winter Notes

Winter is your great opportunity to get your act together. You'll find that once you work out all the details, you'll be even more comfortable than your "civilized" friends in their stuffy, dark, cave-like homes.

If you're set up in an exposed and windy place in the wintertime, you'll want a tight door with all the lacing pins in place *(see "Wall Skin," p. 48, B-6)*. A full liner and a second inner door will stop just about all drafts. A solid wooden door is described in "Old Ways," p. 7.

Three or four ropes tied to the top of the wall frame, up under the roof skin, and then to stakes at the bottom of the wall secure the yurt in the wind *(p. 8, B)*. Under very harsh conditions, you might consider the heavier, nearly impervious felt yurt described in "Traditional Skin," p. 9.

It should be noted that because of its lightness, this frame can't hold a heavy snow load. A broom can be used to gently beat most of the snow off the roof from inside the yurt, while the rest can be swept off from the outside. If you're going to be away for more than a week or two when heavy snow is a possibility, you should set up the *bagana* (the forked poles you used in the yurt erection), and tie them in place before you leave, for extra support, just in case.

Moving the Yurt

This entire yurt weighs under 200 pounds, making a compact load for ox, truck, or station wagon. If you're only moving a short distance, say out of the sun and into the shade for the summer, here's an idea: You (and four or five friends) can carry the whole yurt, frame, and cover to the new site!

To pull off this trick, dismantle the loft (if you have one), taking everything out of the yurt that can't be stepped over easily. You'll also have to put a temporary brace across the bottom of the door, and make sure the rope around the latticework wall is snug, so that the bottom of the yurt can't expand. Remove the smokehole cover, loosen the door posts, and you're ready.

Station yourself and at least five friends around the outside of the yurt. Teamwork, not brute strength, is what's important here. Just all lift on the rope at once and march to the new site, where, if you've planned ahead, you'll find a 13-foot circle scratched on the ground and the door post holes already dug.

Amazing!

LUXURY EXTRAS

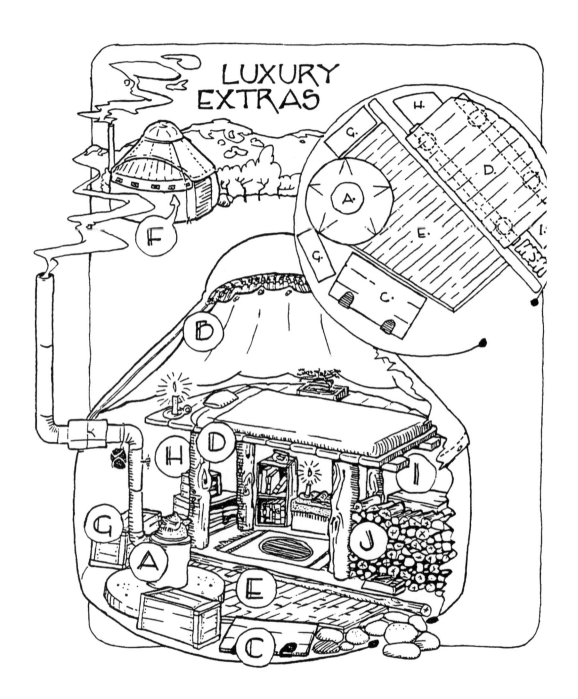

5
LUXURY EXTRAS

A yurt is not a *ger*. Now that you have the basic yurt, ready to move into, perhaps I can interest you in a few little luxury extras to make life more comfortable in your new home. Some are old, some are new. All have been tested in the bush and heartily approved. See also the traditional yurt layout, "Old Ways," p. 2.

Let me say right out front that I prefer the comforts of life, and that even though I consider myself a nomad, my goal is always to be as cozy and protected from the elements as possible.

In this illustration *(opposite)* is my home as it stood in 1980, where the illustrations were originally conceived and drawn:

A. My old stove, not recommended, but cheap
B. Liner from floor to smokehole
C. Refrigerator/root cellar
D. Sleeping loft with library/office/guest bed below
E. Multi-level floor of dirt, stone and wood
F. Solar window for winter warmth

Also shown are areas set aside for kitchen *(G)*, clothes *(H)*, storage *(I)*, and wood *(J)*. Let me explain all of these one at a time, and add a few other little tricks I've found. The refrigerator and the loft are built on-site *before* the yurt is assembled.

Choose those extras which appeal to you. I choose them all, especially on this snowy night in January when I need all the help I can get—and get it, thanks to a little forethought.

But before we begin, a little story . . .

A Magic Night in the Yurt

It's a January night — 2 feet of snow and the stars flashing outside. The latticework of the yurt frame is silhouetted against the canvas, slightly dimmed by the liner inside.

Two burdened shapes are trudging towards the door.

"Hallo!"

"Hola! Come in!"

Candles fill the domed interior with yellow light. After much stomping of boots and many layers of clothing have been hung to dry, hot tea and a pipe are offered and gratefully received.

The little stove makes a muffled roar like the dynamo of a spacecraft, while the instruments are brought out and tuned.

Later, the moon rises high over the dark shapes of the mountains and corn pops in the lantern-like dwelling below. And the songs go on until the wee hours of the morning.

The next day I discover that outside the temperature had dropped to –25° F that magic night.

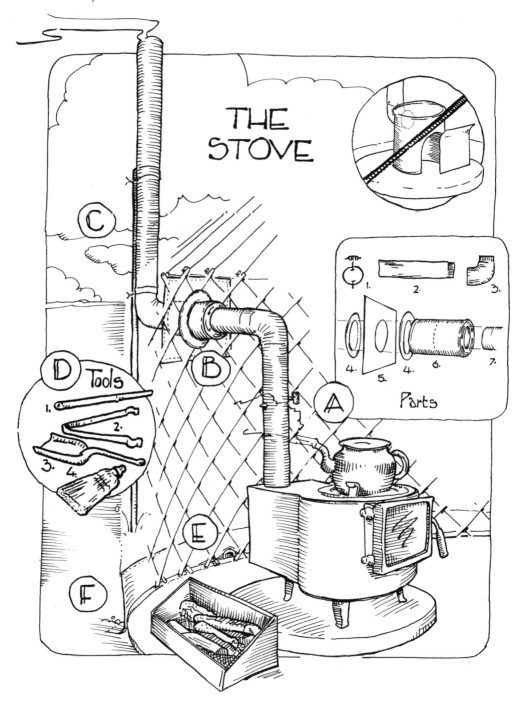

THE STOVE

Parts

Tools

The Stove

My first stove *(opposite, top of the page, with the line through it)* was a 5-gallon can turned upside down with a hole knocked out for a 5-inch stovepipe and an arched door. For your safety, I'll recommend you not use my can stove idea, but it did work for me, at the time. Like so much of my life, when I look back, the only reason I survived, why the stove without a bottom didn't get kicked or bumped over, was dumb luck.

Modern Asian yurt-dwellers put their stove in the middle of the floor for religious as well as practical reasons. Fire is sacred. The stove is placed in the center of the yurt, with the pipe going straight up and out a section of the Gate to Heaven, the *tono*, the smokehole ring. Their stoves usually have an extra chamber between the firebox and the stovepipe, to capture more heat and give a little more stovetop to the cook.

Stovepipe

There are three places where the stovepipe could go through the skin of the yurt: 1) through the wall, 2) through a custom-cut hole in the roof, or 3) the Mongolian way, best if your interior diameter is over 16 feet.

In Mongolia, it's normal to have the stovepipe go straight up and out, through the smokehole ring, the *tono*.

The *tono* has a built-in dome frame, and one panel is fitted with an insulated hole, often just a piece of sheet metal with a stovepipe-sized hole in it. The rest of the *tono* dome is covered and vented as needed, using ropes secured outside the *ger*. Their stoves usually have an extra chamber between the firebox and the stovepipe, to capture more heat and give a little more stovetop to the cook.

The Stove, Really

To your left you'll see a nice stove, and a system for taking the stovepipe safely out the wall. The 3-legged little stove is drawn from one seen on the web, made specifically for "boilers operating on solid fuel, designed for use in private houses and Mongolian felt tents." Manufactured by Zuunnaiman Suvraga Co., Ltd. of Mongolia, from a French design, it may be hard to actually obtain one of these babies, but doesn't it look great?

Many kinds of small wood stoves can be found in catalogs, hardware stores and antique shops, at prices ranging from under twenty dollars for a brand-new tin lizzy type, to hundreds and even thousands for an old gem. Some are more portable than others. See p. 139 for some small stove sources. You may want to try welding one yourself, or having a small stove custom-made. Be sure the size is appropriate to the size of your yurt: Too small and you'll be cold, too large and you'll be using more fuel than necessary, and possibly creating a fire danger.

The most important things are to vent well, to keep stray fumes inside the stove, and not to burn your house down.

Parts (A):

Here are the parts used to safely take the 6-inch stovepipe through the wall:

1. A 6" damper
2. Five straight sections of 6" stovepipe
3. Three 90° angle sections of 6" stovepipe
4. Two trim collars, for outside the canvas and inside the latticework
5. Silcon-coated fiberglass tent flue shield
6. Insulated stovepipe section, 12" long, 10" outside diameter, 6" inside diameter
7. 6" stovepipe
8. About 30 stove screws (not shown)

Because I'm just a single guy, my 13-foot yurt is small by Mongolian standards. I decided that a stove in the middle might be in my way, so I moved it to what would be the men's area (the left side, facing in), near the wall. I set my stove on a mud platform, but you could set it directly on the ground.

The 6-inch-diameter stovepipe goes out near the top of the wall *(B)*, with a 12-inch-long insulated pipe jacket (made by Simpson Dura-Vent) slipped over the section that goes through the wall. The jacket is vented, allowing airflow, with a "ceramic refractory blanket" against the stovepipe. This will protect the latticework frame.

The hole through the tent wall must be carefully placed. I recommend marking the placement of the hole with the wall skin in place. Cut out a 2½-foot square and replace it with fireproof, silicone-coated fiberglass material, making a hole in the center to accommodate the stovepipe with its insulated jacket, usually about 10 inches total diameter. See p. 139 for sources.

Each stovepipe connection should be fastened with at least three stove screws. Outside the yurt, support the stovepipe with a heavy rod or pipe *(C)* pounded into the ground and wired to the stovepipe. The stovepipe should be about 2 feet higher than highest point of the roof, to eliminate the danger of stray sparks coming in contact with the canvas.

By adjusting the air intake and the damper, you can let the fire burn slowly. The stove should be at least 3 feet away from the tent wall, and the place where the stovepipe goes through the roof or wall must be carefully insulated to keep the flammable canvas away from the hot stovepipe.

It's good to make a vent at the bottom of the wall near the stove *(E)* to admit fresh air, replacing the air drawn out of the tent by the stove. Because the wall must come to the ground to insulate from drafts, a strip of waterproof material *(F)* may be added along the bottom edge of the wall skin.

Sims Stoves, as well as others, sell what they call a silicon-coated fiberglass tent flue shield, which you will have to sew into the cover, to safely escort the stovepipe through the roof or wall. See p. 139 for sources.

Fireplace Tools

A few specialized tools *(p. 78, D)* have proven themselves to be of aid in fire building:

1. Hollow blowstick, about 2 feet long
2. Skeenchers, like giant tweezers
3. Coal and ashes shovel
4. Whiskbroom

The hollow blowstick is for blowing a directed stream of air from a comfortable distance. The "skeenchers" are for moving burning wood around. *(Note the ancient Mongolian skeenchers on p. 78.)*

When building a fire in the stove, remember that it needs as much air as wood. Open the damper and stack kindling and small sticks loosely in the bottom of the stove. Ignite this and add small, then larger logs. Logs in this case being split wood about a foot long, and not much bigger around than your forearm. Split wood burns best. You'll find standing deadwood drier and sappier than lying-down deadwood.

OTHER EXTRAS

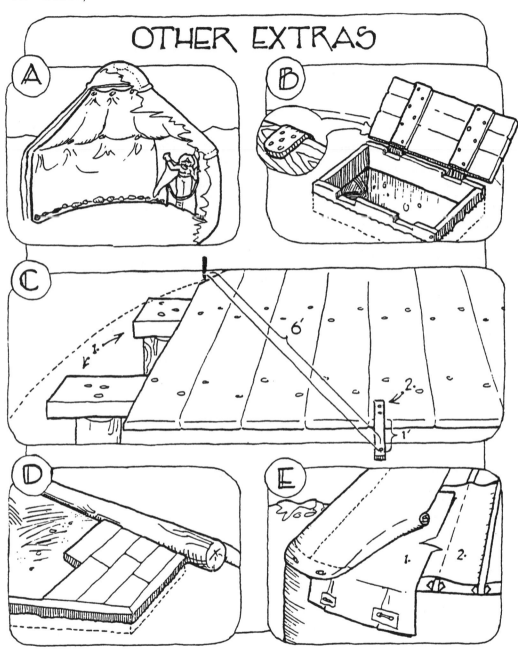

Tips on Staying Warm

Here are a couple of warm tips concerning winter life in the yurt:

Bedwarmer

Heat a flat stone, measuring about 10 inches in diameter and about 3 inches thick on your stove until you can just barely pick it up with your hands; then wrap it in several layers of newspaper, brown paper bags, or a towel; and put at the foot of your bed between the sheets, a little while before retiring. It will heat your bed deliciously, and the rock will still be warm in the morning. I think this is an old cave man invention.

Morning Preparedness

Before going to bed each night, prepare what you need for fire-starting the next morning. That is, kindling, wood and matches should be ready and waiting, so you can leap out of bed, start the fire, and leap back into bed until the yurt warms up a bit.

The Liner

The Liner *(A, opposite)* is an inner wall that helps air circulate in the summer, and creates dead air space insulation when snow piles up outside in the winter, making the yurt easier to heat and keep warm.

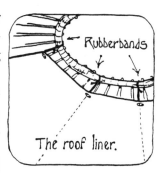

The basic liner is a strip of cloth the same length as the wall, safety-pinned to the wall frame ties at the top, and at the bottom weighted down with rocks, or tucked under the frame rest.

In summer, a liner 3 to 4 feet high will keep ground drafts off you, but in winter, it's good to have as much liner as possible, right up to the smokehole, using any spare blankets or material you have. Safety-pin the top edge of the roof liner to rubber bands tied to the smokehole ring, as shown at right. The bottom edge of the roof liner should go inside the wall part, so that any water will run between the liner and the wall skin.

To keep your bed dry in heavy rains, have a liner over the bed at all times.

Thumbtack the liner to the door posts and, if necessary, add an inside door blanket to stop drafts.

The Refrigerator

Another helpful tip is the hole-in-the-ground refrigerator *(p. 82, B)*, not unlike root cellars of old. Great, both for keeping things cool in summer, and from freezing in winter.

Its size will depend on your needs, which will vary a lot with the seasons. In summer, a 5-gallon can or plastic bucket can be set into the ground below floor level to keep all your perishable food at an ideal, cool temperature.

In wintertime, a deeper hole is desirable. It should be dug well below the frost-line, which is usually 1 to 2 feet below the surface. It should be big enough to accommodate food, water, and anything else you don't want to freeze, such as glue, ink, and toothpaste.

This winter refrigerator is 2 feet wide, 4 feet long, and 4 feet deep. I built a wooden frame of 2 × 6's and a tight cellar door to fit on it. For hinges, I used old shoe soles. The hole can then be lined with wood, or, if the earth seems solid, you can just leave the walls dirt and keep your food and water in airtight buckets in the "cellar."

All food must be stored in tight containers, for protection from forest creatures.

The Loft

The loft *(p. 82, C)* is a platform big enough to sleep on, supported by four posts set in the ground. This arrangement has many assets. It keeps your bed clean, warm and dry, and creates another living space below it. It allows you to stand, looking out from the smoke-hole; and it is useful when erecting, dismantling, or making repairs on the yurt. Like the refrigerator, the loft should be constructed on the site *before* the yurt is assembled.

The four supporting posts are 5 feet long, one foot of which is set into the ground. Redwood or cedar is rot-resistant, and can be placed directly in the soil. If not, the ends can be preserved with creosote, motor oil, or some other sealer. The posts can be lumber or logs, but the top faces must be flat. I do not recommend using treated lumber, since it has been impregnated with toxic bug-killer, and there could be outgassing fumes.

The holes for the two back posts (the two nearest the wall) should be a 1½ feet from the back wall and 5 feet from each other. The front posts are about 6 feet apart and 3 feet from the back ones.

As you set them in the ground, use a board and a bubble level to get the tops of the posts to exactly the same height, before settling the bases by tamping rocks and dirt completely around them.

Nail two 7½-foot beams (of 4 × 4, 2 × 8, or something stronger) across the posts as shown *(p. 82, C-1)*. Put down the floor of the loft, first nailing a 5-foot length of 2 × 6's across the exact centers of the loft beams so that the back edge is 6 inches from where the yurt wall will be. This is the widest part of the loft.

Find a scrap piece of wood about a foot-and-a-half long and pound a nail part way in near one end of it. With this nail sticking up, pound this scrap into the first floorboard of the loft, so that the nail is one foot out from the front edge of the loft *(p. 82, C-2)*. Over the nail, hook a 6-foot-long string looped at both ends. This is your guide for sawing the round, back edge of the loft.

Add the rest of the floorboards (I used 2 × 4 pieces of varying length), lining up their front edges with the first board. Mark the back edge for sawing with a pencil in the string guide.

On top of this sturdy platform you can lay a mattress or foam pad and bedding.

The Floor

A plain dirt or mud floor is fairly easy to keep clean, and entirely adequate for short-term camps. This floor can be covered with plastic tarps and rugs to keep the ground moisture and cold out.

For a more permanent site, you can take the time to lay a nice stone or wood floor. In New Mexico, there's a history of hard adobe floors of mud and straw, hardened with ox or pig blood, or linseed oil cut with kerosene — overkill, unless this is to be a permanent site.

A simple but beautiful wood floor *(p. 82, D)* can be laid with 2 × 4 mill ends obtained for little or nothing from your local sawmill. Since they are usually cut of planed lumber, no finishing (other than a sealer) is necessary after the floor is down.

Level the floor *(see "Preparing the Site," p. 63)*, and frame the area with 2 × 4's set in the ground with the "two-inch" side up. Wet the dirt inside the frame thoroughly, so that mud will ooze into the cracks between the wood blocks, for a snug fit.

My own floor was a combination of all three: the guest bed (under the loft) being a dirt floor covered with plastic, a foam pad, and blankets; the doorway of stone; and the living area in front of the stove, of wood blocks.

The Solar Window

A solar window *(p. 82, E)* delivers light and warmth even on the coldest clear days. The window pictured here uses a double layer of weather-resistant plastic, transparent or translucent, on the southern part of the yurt roof, and does not involve cutting the canvas roof. I used a 6-by-12-foot piece of the heaviest-gauge vinyl sold by my local lumber dealer.

Make the window by unpinning part of the roof skin, and tightly folding the lower edge of the roof cover under (uncut), to the desired height for the top of the window. Then mark the arc of the window's top edge with a permanent pen, roughly, by laying the vinyl over the hole. Cut the arc in the vinyl with a scissors or utility knife. Tuck the top long edge of the soft window material up under the rolled canvas roof. This makes an arc (in this case from door to stovepipe) about 12 feet across and 3 feet high in the middle.

The outside layer of plastic *(p. 82, E-1)* goes under the roof skin and over the wall skin for shedding water. I safety-pinned the plastic to the canvas, having first reinforced the plastic inside and out with duct tape. For the bottom part of the plastic to fit tightly to the wall, you'll have to put folds at each safety pin.

The inside layer of plastic *(p. 82, E-2)* is laced over and under the rafters for an insulating, pillow effect. It goes up as far as the outside piece of plastic and down to the top of the wall.

In summer, this window can be moved to the north or east side of the yurt roof for light but no extra heat.

Now that you're all settled in, with all the conveniences that make life worthwhile, I feel obligated to fill you in on another aspect of tent life that you may have to face at some point:

Rip-Offs

Back in Mongolia, every *ger* has a dog, and vice versa. It's impolite to knock before entering the *ger* because it implies that your host is less than hospitable. The proper greeting when approaching a *ger* in Mongolia is *"Nohkoi khor!"* or, "Hold the dog!"

Also, the *gers* of Eastern Asia are quite heavy, made of hardwood, and covered in many layers of felt with a massive, lockable door.

Everyone is susceptible to burglary, but living without locks increases the risk. There's nothing more aggravating than discovering yourself a victim, and, not knowing who the culprit is, being helpless to recover the goods or even just look da bugga in the eye. Suspicion and anger you didn't think yourself capable of can surface.

I've had my yurt on maybe 15 sites over the years under many circumstances, and been "invaded" four or five times. Generally these seem to have been the work of young kids, judging by the things they were attracted to: money, pot, small shiny objects, etc.

An extremely inaccessible location, or one close to friends (nomads or otherwise), cuts down the risk, but of course there is no absolute protection. It's sad to think that anyone would do anything like that to *you*, but I've found that the experience need not be entirely unprofitable.

After the initial anger and tension are worn away (climb a mountain, jump in the river) there comes some feeling of the transitory nature of *everything* and perhaps a little more appreciation of how good you've got it right now, hmmm?

Tipi *vs. Ger*

When nomads gather, the topic of tipi vs. *ger*/yurt may surface. It's a circular argument. Both are functional and beautiful; the pros and cons balance out. Choose the lodge that best fits your situation and personality.

The straightforwardness of the tipi, its pyramidal shape, and the feeling of infinity inside looking up at the apex of the cone, make this Native American design a masterpiece. Because of the slope of the roof, the tipi can shed rain and handle a snow load better than a yurt.

On the other hand, the basket-like frame of the *ger* culminates at the smokehole, the crown, the *tono*. A low ceiling makes it easy to heat and the short poles fit on or in most vehicles. The straight walls of the yurt give you as much head space as floor space, unlike the tipi.

As some kind of comparison, this drawing shows outlines of an 18-foot tipi and a 13-foot yurt, both using the same amount of cover material (33 yards, 6 feet wide).

Tipi and *ger* are as different as west and east. It's also worth mentioning that the *ger*-dwelling nomads of the ancient East had access to vast flat areas for fairly easy migration, domestic livestock for meat, milk, felt and other textiles, the wheel, and access to the great trade routes, allowing them to refine their designs over generations, using contemporary technologies.

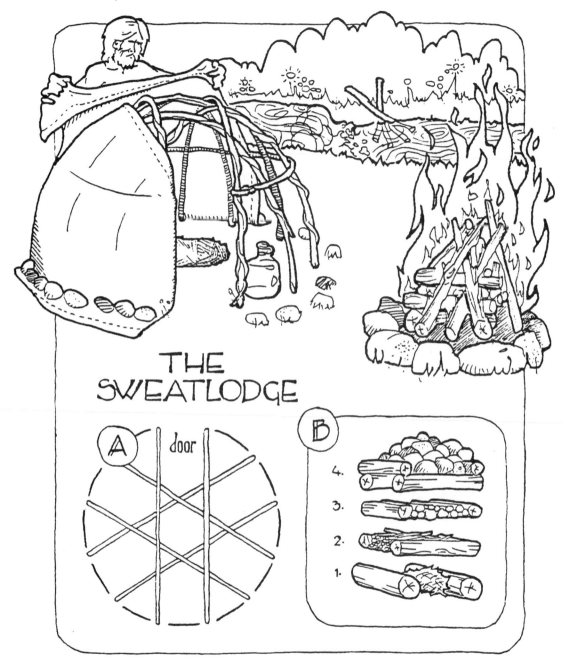

THE SWEATLODGE

A door

B

4.

3.

2.

1.

The Sweatlodge

The Native American lifestyle and specifically the tipi were major sources for my research on the nomadic way. I lived in a tipi while constructing this yurt and it was inspirational. I learned about open fires in a tipi and my door design is a direct carryover from the canvas tipi.

Another aspect of the Indian Way, and one which I doubt is practiced in the Gobi Desert or anywhere else in Mongolia for that matter, is the sweatlodge *(opposite)*.

A very efficient way to keep clean, and a spiritual purification, the sweatlodge is a steambath conducted in a small, blanket-covered framework of willows. When you can stand no more, you step outside and rinse with cold water, that can be anything from a garden hose to a waterfall, pond, river, etc.

The Site

Choose a spot for the sweatlodge close to some kind of water, if possible, and with a large-enough clearing to build a roaring fire. Make a boulder border around the fireplace about 4 feet in diameter.

Prepare the leveled lodge site by digging a pit about a foot across and a foot deep, using the dirt to make a path to the fireplace. The pit should be clean of any roots or dead grass, which would smoke.

Mark twelve points on a 6-foot circle centered around the pit, evenly spaced from each other. These twelve markers (use small stones) indicate where the butt ends of the arched poles will be pushed into the ground.

The Framework

The framework of the sweatlodge is made from fifteen straight green willows, about the thickness of your thumb at the base and about 10 feet long. Trim them of branches and sharpen the bottom ends of twelve of them.

Push these poles (the pointed ends) into the ground at the marked places around the pit. Especially if the earth is rocky or hard, a piece of rebar or pipe can be driven in first, to make a hole for the pole.

Once all the poles are in the ground, make arches with pairs by twisting them around each other. The diagram in *(A)* shows how to pair the poles so that a 6-pointed star is formed. The poles should be long enough to reach almost to each others' bases to make a well-rounded lodge.

Each place where the poles cross should be tied, either with bark from the willows or string. Choose a large door opening in the framework facing the fireplace. Leaving this space open, tie the remaining poles to make a ring horizontally about halfway up on the outside of the lodge. These will add strength and provide more room inside by keeping the cover from sagging.

Rocks

The rocks must be chosen carefully as the wrong kind may explode in the fire or, worse, in the lodge. Although this has never happened to me, it's not unheard-of.

They should be gathered from a hillside and *not* from a riverbed. Granite and other kinds that flake or sparkle in the sun — *forget it.* The ideal rocks are volcanic and it's easy to spot their dull, dark, porous surfaces.

Choose rocks about the size of your two clenched fists and pile about fifteen of them near the fireplace.

Forked Sticks

Cut two forked sticks of dead wood about 4 feet long with 6-inch forks. These are for transporting the hot rocks from the fire to the sweatlodge.

If possible, until you need them, keep the forked ends under water.

The Fire

The fire is built *outside* the sweatlodge. Firewood is cut to about 3-foot lengths with diameters of 6 inches and less. The fire is built so that the rocks are heated from underneath first, then fall onto a bed of coals. The fire is illustrated on p. 88 *(B)*.

First lay your two largest logs down inside the rock-bordered fireplace, parallel to and about a foot and a half from each other *(p. 88, B-1)*. Between them place the kindling. Put two more logs on top of and crossing the first two, and small sticks between *(B-2),* then a layer of small logs *(B-3)*. On top of this, make a square of four logs and carefully pile the rocks in the resulting nest *(B-4)*.

Finally, cover it all with the rest of the wood.

About one hour before you want to sweat, light the fire on the side that the wind is coming from.

Covering the Lodge

While the fire is burning, you can cover the lodge. Ten to twelve blankets will make the sweatlodge fairly airtight, some or all of which can be replaced with a tarpaulin.

Final Preparations

Now, while the fire is still burning, collect cedar, sage, eucalyptus, mullein, or whatever other aromatic plant may be available where you live and put a few bunches inside the door of the lodge (or, you can cover the whole floor with green sprigs to sit on).

Fill two containers with water, one for drinking and one for rinsing and pouring on the rocks. If you want something to sit on, small logs or large woodblocks work fine, but when the water hits the rocks, the air will be cooler closer to the ground.

The Sweat

When the fire has burned down to coals, retrieve your two forked sticks and use them to carry the hot rocks from the fireplace to the sweatlodge pit (as demonstrated here). The rocks should be red hot, so be careful.

All right! Take off your clothes. Before you get into the lodge, you might want to get wet. This will make the heat more tolerable, be gentler on your hair, and sort of prime the pump, allowing perspiration to flow more freely.

A lodge this size can hold as many as eight friends, six casual acquaintances or four total strangers.

Close the door tightly. You might want to sit in the dry heat for a while before watering the rocks as your eyes adjust to the dark. If you heated the rocks properly, some of them will still be glowing, like the eyes of a dragon waiting in the dark.

Sprinkle water on the rocks a little at a time, and if the heat seems too intense, breathe through some sage or get nearer the floor where the air is cooler. Once you get used to it, you'll be surprised at how much you can take.

If you collected aromatic herbs as mentioned, you can place some on the rocks (after they've cooled a bit) and wet them to produce lung-cleansing vapor.

Some like to go out and rinse a few times during a sweat, while others like to sit out the whole thing, leaving only when the rocks have quit sizzling and no more steam can be had.

The sensation of awareness, clean-ness, and alive-ness when standing in the sunshine after a sweat can only be experienced, and I won't even attempt to describe it.

YURT MADNESS

A — Spare room

B — Hot tub room

C — Greenhouse

D — Camp tent

6
NEW WAYS

Now you've learned a little about traditional yurt-dwellers, and seen in detail how my own yurt is set up. This chapter will delve into the further evolution of yurts and yurt-like objects in the modern world. We'll also look at a couple of completely different tents that could be made with little difficulty or expense. There are many more yurt variations, too, at the back of the book.

Yurt Madness

In the United States, variations on the basic yurt design reflect American ingenuity and affluence. This drawing *(opposite)* illustrates just a few of the applications this versatile structure is finding in the modern western culture.

Spare Room
As a spare room *(A)*, the yurt is a place for the kids, a guest room, or just a private sanctuary for meditation, yoga, music, drawing, or writing.

Hot Tub Room
With a little stove and an open or see-through skylight, the yurt is a perfect housing for your hot tub *(B)*. Private, aesthetic, and you won't have to give up your garage.

Greenhouse
In this version, about one-third of the canvas is replaced with clear or translucent vinyl two layers thick *(C)*, to greatly extend your growing season. With the two roof supports in place you can hang many plants from the smokehole ring. Water barrels painted flat black will store heat through the night.

Camp Tent
For the weekend nomad, a smaller-sized yurt (8-to-10-foot diameter) can easily be carried even on the smallest vehicles *(D)*.

Nylon-reinforced vinyl skins covering bones of planed lumber, and joined with nuts and bolts, are very popular with the yurt makers of this country. Permanent yurts and yurts within yurts appear suddenly in the woods like visitors from another galaxy. Peek into pp. 94–96, for a glimpse into the range of possibilities.

Other Nomad Homes

Here are two more great alternatives that might appeal to the nomad of little means. Both are based on simple geometric forms: The first *(A, opposite)* is a half-sphere and resembles the wigwam of the Native Americans who live in the Great Lakes region and eastward; the second *(B)* is three-fourths of an icosahedron and looks like a huge crystal, similar in design to the tents of the northern Siberian nomads.

Daydreams & Fantasies

The half-sphere dome tent and the icosatent are just ideas that I've had. I haven't built them, but they seem fairly simple and perhaps they'll inspire the more creative nomads to invent their own tents. Both of these former daydreams are being manufactured right now by businesses listed at the back of the book.

The Dome Tent

The Dome Tent *(A—see the similar Alachigh tent made by Steve Place and Francine Isaacs on p. 134)* is like a large version of the Smokehole Cover *(p. 54)*. It has a central ring with a built-in dome that can be covered with a heavy tarp or blanket. In this particular vision, it's also got an open fire, a liner, and a tipi-style door.

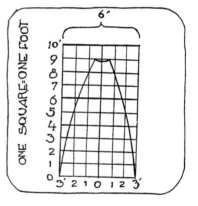

The pattern provided here will result in a 15-foot diameter half-sphere. Copy the pattern eight times onto 6-foot-wide canvas. (This will take about 30 yards.)

Sew these eight pieces together. On the last seam make a tipi-style door with grommets for five or six lacing pins. The hole at the top will be about 2½ feet in diameter and should have a border like the door.

The frame shown here *(A-1)* is made of sixteen green poles at least 20 feet long, set about 2 feet into the ground, equally spaced in a 15-foot-diameter circle. The poles are curved into four sets of parallel arches, to make an 8-pointed star at the top *(A-2)*. To further support the skin and strengthen the bones, more green sticks are braced inside the framework.

Then the cover is thrown on and staked down, and the poles of the frame stretched tightly against the canvas. Arrange the poles so that the smokehole on the skin matches up with the corresponding hole in the center of the 8-pointed star in the bones. Tie all the intersections on the frame. A willow hoop with the smokehole dome attached is lashed to the top of the frame.

Because of its slanting roof, this is a good design to use with a sunken floor, if the Earth permits.

The Icosatent

Tents very similar to this Icosatent can be found in the "Suppliers" section on p. 136.

An icosahedron is the smallest spheroid you can make using equilateral triangles. It's one of the five platonic solids, having twenty equalateral triangle faces, thirty edges, and twelve vertices!

The Icosatent *(B, p. 94)* is three-quarters of an icosahedron. Five triangles have been removed from the bottom, leaving fifteen — that is, ten in the walls and five in the roof. In a way, the Icosatent is the simplest possible yurt, with ten wall poles and five rafters.

The cover is made of fifteen equilateral triangles of material. Circular patches at the corners will make the sewing easier. Use a double-lap seam *(shown on p. 48, B)*, sewing the roof first. A skylight of heavy-gauge plastic, folded to the proper cone, could be sewn on at the peak. Be sure that the seam at the bottom of the skylight and the seam connecting roof and wall overlap so that they'll shed water. The roof and the bottom of the wall especially should be waterproofed.

For a door, any one of the wall seams can be equipped with a zipper. The bottom hem of the cover should be tripled and grommets installed at each corner.

There are twenty-five struts in the frame, and eleven hubs *(p. 94, B-1)*. The length of the struts, of course, will determine the size of the tent.

The possibilities for strut and hub material boggle the mind. Here are three that came to me long ago. The best and strongest hubs for a wood-framed icosahedral structure are steel sections of 3-inch pipe, connected with stainless steel strap (using a lumber-strapping tool) through holes drilled in the ends of struts. *See p. 136 of* Shelter *(referenced in the bibliography on p. 129).*

In any case, the frame will have to be staked down at each of the five hubs at ground level. Extra roof poles radiating from the top center hub would buoy up the large expanses of otherwise unsupported canvas.

The Way of the Nomad Today

Because of the freedom that we've been given, particularly in this country at this time, it seems as if each person is a little culture unto him or herself. Those who veer off the course laid out so carefully by our "programmers" (TV, newspapers, movies, etc.) are likely to arrive at totally unique lifestyles. Now that we have access to cultures living in the world, as well as the great civilizations that have existed in the past, there's almost limitless reference material to draw upon.

While the new nomad is without the ancient culture and experience of the true nomad, he's not completely unprepared. As common sense dictates, and his own needs and wants become apparent, the tent-dweller's tent and way of life will become more and more comfortable and distinctive.

The nomad is free to follow the winds of change and even feels a certain security in that instability. The clutches of debt, the rut of "nine-to-five," and the confinement of four walls are successfully eluded. The concept of land ownership seems slightly absurd to a nomad, whose front yard changes completely with every move.

It's a life close to the earth, as close to the elements of Nature as you can get, and yet still feeling protected from Her more extreme moods. The sound of the river, the wind in the trees, birdsong, and approaching visitors are all audible from your living room. You know where your wood and water come from, and you know where your garbage goes. Life is clean and simple.

The nomad isn't always a sheepherder (or a struggling author/artist/musician). Any occupation in which you live by your integrity, dealing directly with those interested in your services, will do. You could be a dancer or a tailor, a gypsy or a magician, an adventurer or a pilgrim, a woodcarver or a yurtbuilder, a tourist or a farmer. It's your world!

What Next?

I have the urge to travel, someday, to the East. To Japan, to learn the fine art of bamboo craft; and to Mongolia, to study with the *ger* makers there.

I'm a nomad for life. There's much to learn about climates, elevations, and locations, getting along with the neighbors, living in comfort, and traveling light. If I can pass anything of use along as I learn, then it's all worth it, yes?

BACK OF THE BOOK

Appendices

Suppliers

OTHER SIZES

GENERAL DIMENSIONS

Diameter	13'	16'	16'	19'
Height	10'	12'	9'	10'
Roof angle	45°	45°	30°	30°

SKIN

Canvas (6' wide)	33 yds	41 yds	38 yds	49 yds
Circumference	42'6"	51'9"	51'9"	61'4"
Roof overhang	6"	6"	7"	8"
For the roof ptrn:	LONG STRING	9'8"	12'	9'9"	11'7"
	SHORT STRING	2'10"	2'8"	2'4"	2'4"
No. roof pieces	8	10	10	12

BONES

No. wall sections	4	5	5	6
No. rafters	45	55	55	65
Rafter length	7'	9'	7'6"	9'

Other Sizes I & II

For one person, a 13-foot yurt as described in the first part of this book is plenty of room, easy to heat, and very portable. A couple, a family, or one person needing more space might consider either another yurt, or a larger size.

In this updated and expanded version of *Mongolian Cloud Houses*, I'm including the original, unedited, **Other Sizes I** *(opposite)*. I'm just playing with some of the possibilities here—the larger sizes, in particular, have *not* been built.

Other Sizes II, displays the numbers I used for my most recent yurt, based on more recent research into design and techniques.

Other Sizes I

The chart opposite provides the numbers you'll need to build a yurt of either a 16- or 19-foot diameter. On the 16-foot model, I offer the choice of a 45° or 35° roof angle. A higher roof allows lots of room for a loft and will shed rain and snow better than a lower roof.

A lower roof is easier to heat, but requires more support. The *bagana*, the forked poles used in assembling the yurt *("Putting It All Together," p. 61),* will probably have to remain in place. A larger yurt will need proportionately thicker poles.

While the chart lists changes in the plans, some statistics will remain the same for all sizes in this section, Other Sizes I. These are:

1. The wall height (6 feet),
2. The door hole on the skin,
3. The individual latticework wall sections,
4. The door frame, and
5. The smokehole ring diameter (4 feet).

Other Sizes II

In rediscovering the *ger* design, many solutions have come to me that now seem obvious. *(See "Bones II," p. 31.)* There is still a lot of work to be done. Most of the changes are equally applicable to solid or hollow-pole yurts, and all are meant to make life easier for yurt-builders.

The door described in "Bones II, *Nars*" *(p. 43)* is bamboo-only. As an alternate door design, I'd suggest something closer to the door shown in "Old Ways," p. 6, *(B).* The bamboo yurt is still a possibility, but bamboo must be kept dry.

The following two pages are meant to put all the information for one size in one place.

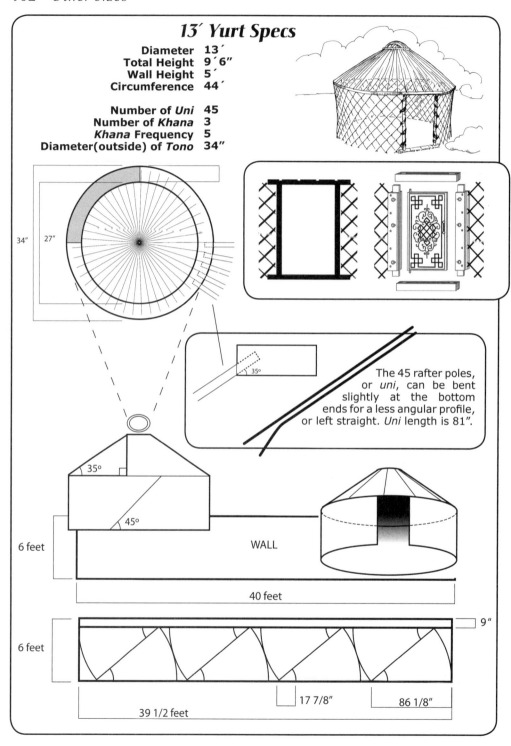

13′ Yurt Specs

Diameter	**13′**
Total Height	**9′6″**
Wall Height	**5′**
Circumference	**44′**
Number of *Uni*	**45**
Number of *Khana*	**3**
***Khana* Frequency**	**5**
Diameter(outside) of *Tono*	**34″**

34″ 27″

35°

The 45 rafter poles, or *uni*, can be bent slightly at the bottom ends for a less angular profile, or left straight. *Uni* length is 81″.

35°

45°

6 feet

WALL

40 feet

9″

6 feet

17 7/8″ 86 1/8″

39 1/2 feet

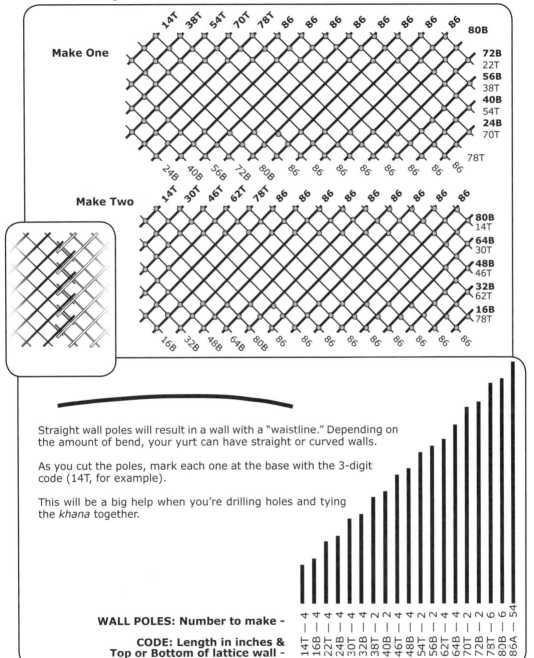

Straight wall poles will result in a wall with a "waistline." Depending on the amount of bend, your yurt can have straight or curved walls.

As you cut the poles, mark each one at the base with the 3-digit code (14T, for example).

This will be a big help when you're drilling holes and tying the *khana* together.

	14T	16B	22T	24B	30T	32B	38T	40B	46T	48B	54T	56B	62T	64B	70T	72B	78T	80B	85A
WALL POLES: Number to make -	4	4	4	4	4	4	2	2	4	4	2	4	4	2	2	6	6	54	

CODE: Length in inches & Top or Bottom of lattice wall -

Yurt Scrapbook
1976–2005

1979

In those days they called me Dan the Jan, 12-string Dan, even Yurt Dan, but never Dulcimer Dan, that's another Dan . . .

Five summers and three winters, in over a dozen locations around northern New Mexico, often with tipi neighbors . . .

Above, I've removed the cover to air everything out, on a warm spring day in 1978.

1979

1976

1980

1978

Evolution
My yurt, myself…

The yurt kit, spiralling counterclockwise from the center: smokehole ring & cover, khana, uni, *canvas cover, door frame, and* bagana

The site prepared, with luxury extras in place: outwardly slanted frame rest, loft, wood floor, refrigerator hole, stove platform, and even a small wood cache

All tied together with inner tube rubber bands!

Wall and door frame in place

Instrument-maker & neighbor Dennis Dillon, assisting from atop the sleeping loft. Note the two bagana *are set aside, thanks to Dennis, with just five rafter poles in place.*

Yurt "land host" Larry Taub and friends inspecting the finished "bones" of the yurt

Pictured on these two pages is a 1980 yurt built for Bruce Grossman and Susan Berman, paying for my first (18-year) Maui vacation. Photos show erection of the smokehole ring and roof rafters. At bottom right, the frame, complete, then covered.

Luxury extras include the solar window, above, and the hole-in-the-ground refrigerator (bottom of this page).

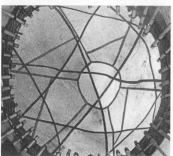

The two images above show the domed smokehole cover removed, and in place. Note the woven willow smokehole ring with fitted tubes for each rafter.

The rafters are adjustable at the bottom ends, because they're tied with flexible inner tube rubber.

Above: keeping food cool in summer and unfrozen in winter

The bamboo yurt aviary kit. A half-inch wire mesh mouse ground barrier is held down by the frame rest—a ring of cinder blocks. Leaning on a bird-perch plant is the laminated fir tono with built-in bamboo dome frame, next the two bagana. The bamboo door frame leans aganst a coco palm trunk, behind the three khana sections.

The bamboo frame, out in the open for clarity. Note the slightly concave waistline, resulting from only slightly curved poles. The as-yet-unrealized plan is to drape aviary netting from the inside...

The *Gers* of Mongolia

Photographs by Jim Macey

The ger of a wealthy businessman set up on a grassy plain during the national horse races eight miles from Mongolia's capital city of Ulaanbaatar

While engaged in geologic field reconnaissance of an unmapped earthquake fault in northwestern Mongolia, we met a local family camped for the summer in their ger *with their herds of sheep and goats.*

Mongolian and American geology students help set up the "kitchen ger" as part of an undergraduate geologic research field camp in the northern Mongolian Altai during the summer of 2004 (above and across opposite page).

One day in September of 2005 during a research expedition investigating the regional tectonics of Mongolia's southern Gobi Desert, a man on horseback suddenly appeared in our midst. He invited us to his ger located faraway in the distance, and let us ride his camels. Here, Jim and Naraa return from a ride.

An interior view of an elaborate ger positioned for the annual Naadam horse races

A seasonal camp in the south central Gobi Desert of Outer Mongolia. The ger is home to a family of five people subsisting on their herds of sheep and goats. During the night I was there, a wolf killed a sheep and ate its tail.

This bag made of animal skin is used to make airag—fermented mare's milk.

Two families with their gers and camels camped in the south central Gobi Desert of Outer Mongolia. Camels provide transportation, sustenance, and the ability to transport gers on a seasonal basis.

Distilling "milk vodka": As the milk below comes to a slow boil, the vapors condense on the metal bowl above and drip into the bucket, providing the family with a mildly alcoholic "milk vodka."

A ger situated on the high summer pastures of the northern Mongolian Altai Mountains. This photo was taken in July. Soon the families, using camels to transport their camps, will migrate in long caravans of animals to lower elevations in the foothills bordering the vast desert plain to the east.

A man named Jamuke, a friend of my friend/host, portraying Genghis Khan in a BBC television documentary. Photo taken on site in 2004 east of Ulaanbaatar.

People of the *Ger*

Photographs by Jim Macey

About photographer Jim Macey

I live in a small Owens Valley town located between Mt. Whitney in the high Sierras and Death Valley. The area is popular with academic geology groups conducting earth science research. In the early 80's when I first began to build a homestead on the Owens Lake sand dunes, geology professors from Humboldt State University joined with me and helped develop the logistics to support a nearby geology field camp.

In 2000, one of the geologists asked me if I could arrange a cultural exchange between Mongolian horsemen and American cowboys. They knew I worked with cowboys packing mules in the Sierras. The geologists had been researching aspects of Central Asian glacial history, working mostly in Mongolia. During their annual field trips they had become familiar with the rural culture of the Mongolian nomads.

I then brought the concept of presenting the Mongolian horse culture to the Western Folklife Center (WFC) in Elko, Nevada, where I had previously worked on a ranch. The WFC produces the annual National Cowboy Poetry Gathering, which often features cowboys from other parts of the world.

Later in 2000, a geology professor and I hosted a delegation of Mongolian academics and met with the WFC in Elko. During the summer of 2001, I was invited to accompany the geology professors on their research expedition to northwest Mongolia where I met with the horsemen I would soon be working with. My role on the trip was to arrange cultural exchange and document the nomadic culture. In June 2002, I visited the Folklife Center in Elko with a group of Mongolian horsemen.

The WFC presented the traditional Mongolian horse culture to a very enthusiastic audience in January 2004 during the poetry gathering. A *ger* was set up in the snow outside the convention center, and marmots were roasted by the Mongolian nomads in exchange with the local Shoshones. Visits were conducted to area schools and ranches accompanied by traditional music. The event was a huge success and took everyone by surprise.

Since then I have traveled with Mongolian and American geologists to other regions of Mongolia: the northern Mongolian Altai Mountains in July 2004 and the Gobi Desert in the fall of 2005. On each trip, I shot pictures of the people and their nomadic dwellings.

—Jim Macey

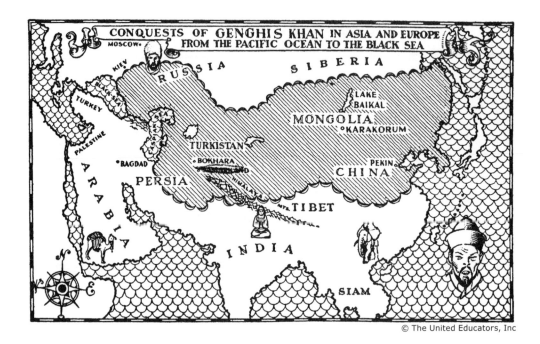

The Drawings of Donn P. Crane

Genghis Khan Conquers Asia

from EXPLORATIONS, Part I, MY BOOK OF HISTORY

A Picturesque Tale of Progress, Volume 7, by Olive Beaupré Miller

Part of a popular children's book series in the 30's, the following images were designed to stimulate learning in young readers. Obviously a great deal of research has gone into their creation. I found them at the Harwood Foundation public library in Taos in the late 70's, and instantly wanted to be a *ger*-dwelling nomad.

These illustrations, by Donn P. Crane, are from *Marco Polo Explores the East,* and *Genghis Khan Conquers Asia,* in that multi-volume visual feast, the out-of-print *The Story of Mankind: A Picturesque Tale of Progress.* All images are copyrighted by The United Educators, Inc.

*We leap back in time, to 1162 and the humble beginnings of the **Genghis Khan** (the title means Great Chieftan), back when he was **Temujin**.*

For centuries the ger *was virtually the only form of housing in Central Asia, other than Buddhist monasteries. "Yurt" is the word the Russians gave to the tents of the Mongolians, but in Mongolia, the word* ger *simply means "dwelling."*

Notice the ger *cover lashings and the way the rug door is tucked up.*

Compare the size and shape of the two gers on this page In the ger *below, it looks like the walls are more vertical than in the exterior views.*

In this drawing, Temujin is choosing his wife. He's 13, she's 9. The fathers seem to approve.

Temujin's wedding day. The distinctive upward swoop of the tono *on the* gers *seen in these drawings is historically accurate, although rarely seen in Central Asia these days.*

In the days of Genghis Khan, the indoor fire was kept in an open brazier, requiring the extra chimney effect of that top nipple to help the smoke out. In a wind, the tono *would be covered on the windward side. The bindings on the outside of the* ger *are also accurate, but there would be no stakes pounded into the ground, as Shamanic taboos forbid any disturbance of the Earth.*

This is a captured Temujin being freed by a "friendly enemy."

"A magnificent palace of marble stood within the park, but the Great Khan was not there. He was at his Royal Pavilion deep in a wooded grove. As the little band approached, they saw that this pavilion was lightly built of bamboo, gilded and beautifully finished. It had gilded and laquered columns, carved in the form of dragons whose heads and outspread claws supported the graceful roof. This building was held in place by two hundred cords of silk and could be taken down and put together wherever the Khan might wish. *At last the Polos entered the presence of the Great Khan!"*

from EXPLORATIONS, Part I, MY BOOK OF HISTORY
A Picturesque Tale of Progress, Volume 7, by Olive Beaupré Miller
©The United Educators, Inc.

Genghis Khan's grandson, Kublai Khan, two generations later, was still a nomad, ruling the vast Mongol Empire from a glorified tent!

The two drawings on this page depict the legendary wheeled gers first described by Rubruquis (c. 1215–1270), a Franciscan friar and medieval traveler. He measured the distance betwen the wheel ruts left by one of those carts — 20 feet!

Being mobile homes, they had sometimes windows for the family inside to enjoy the view. This mode of transport is now obsolete.

Further Research

Video

The Story of the Weeping Camel

Directed by Byambasuren Davaa & Luigi Falorni (85 minutes, 2005)
ThinkFilm, National Geographic World Films (www.weepingcamelmovie.com)
Writing credits: Byambasuren Davaa & Luigi Falorni

When a Mongolian nomadic family's newest camel colt is rejected by its mother, a musician is needed for a ritual to change her mind.

Mujaan

(25 minutes, 2005), DVD, including Elements of Mujaan — six 3-minute shorts by Amy Reed
Custom Flix (mujaan.com)
Commentary Tracks — with archaeologist Jeannine Davis-Kimball, editor Adam Heller & producer Chris McKee 12-page insert with three classroom lessons & information about Mongolia

"This is a beautiful film of rural life in Mongolia. Carefully constructed and thoughtfully paced, it really conveys the essence of what is today almost an ideal — the herding family's calm existence."

–Professor Caroline Humphrey, Cambridge University, UK

Nature: The Wild Horses of Mongolia

(55 minutes, 2002)

"Julia Roberts travels to Mongolia in search of the Asiatic wild horse — the Takhi. In recent times these horses have nearly been hunted to extinction, but now the Mongolian people are re-introducing the Takhis to their natural habitat."

Magazines

National Geographic Magazine

October 1927 *By Coolie and Caravan Across Central Asia*, by William J. Morden
November 1932 *From the Mediterranean to the Yellow Sea by Motor,* by Maynard Williams
June 1933 *Explorations in the Gobi Desert*, by Roy Chapman Andrews
January 1936 *With the Nomads of Central Asia*, by Edward Murray
November 1950 *We Took the High Road in Afghanistan*, by Jean and Franc Shor
November 1954 *How the Kazakhs Fled to Freedom*, by Milton J. Clark
March 1962 *Journey to Outer Mongolia*, by William O. Douglas and Dean Conger
April 1972 *Winter Caravan to the Roof of the World*, by Roland and Sabrina Michaud
November 1973 *The Turkomans, Horsemen of the Steppes*, by Roland and Sabrina Michaud
March 1980 *Journey to China's Far West*, by Rick Gore and Bruce Dale
May 1993 *Mongolian Nomads*, by Cynthia Beall and Melvyn Goldstein
December 1996 *Ghenghis Khan*, by Mike Edwards and James L. Stanfield
February 1997 *The Great Khans*, by Mike Edwards and James L. Stanfield
More at www.nationalgeographic.com

Books

Afghanistan: An Atlas of Indigenous Domestic Architecture
Albert Szabo and Thomas J. Barfield (University of Texas Press, 1991)

Around the Sacred Sea: Mongolia and Lake Baikal on Horseback
Bartle Bull (London: Canongate Books, 2000)

The Book of Bamboo:
A Comprehensive Guide to This Remarkable Plant, Its Uses, and Its History
David Farrelly (Sierra Club Books, 1995)

Build a Yurt: The Low-Cost Mongolian Round House
Len Charney (Macmillan, 1974)

Building in Your Backyard
Victor Lane (Workman Publications, 1979)

Caravans to Tartary
Roland and Sabrina Michaud (Thames & Hudson, 1990)

Circle Houses: Yurts, Tipis and Benders
David Pearson (Chelsea Green, 2001)

The Complete Yurt Handbook
Paul King (Eco-Logic Books, 2002)

Edge of Blue Heaven: A Journey Through Mongolia
Benedict Allen (London: Parkwest Publications, 1999)

Felt: New Directions for an Ancient Craft
Gunilla Paetau Sjoberg, Patricia Spark (Translator) (Interweave Press, 1996)

A Handmade Life
William Coperthwaite (Chelsea Green, 2003)

Home Work
Lloyd Kahn (Shelter Publications, 2004)

How To Build a Portable Yurt
Charles Crawford
(Cascade Shelter, 4500 Aster Street, Springfield, OR 97477)

Igloos, Yurts and Totem Poles:
Life and Customs of Thirteen Peoples Around the Globe
Friedrich Boer, translated from the German by Florence McHugh (Pantheon, 1957)

Mongolia: The Legacy of Chinggis Khan
339 pp. (Thames and Hudson, and Asian Art Museum of San Francisco, 1995)

The Portable Yurt:
A Timeless Home from the Plains of Mongolia Adapted for the Modern Nomad
Chuck and Laurel Cox (Frog Pond Publishers, Lee, NH, 1974)

The Real Mongol *Ger* Book
Froit, the Netherlands, no publisher, but will custom-print
www.nooitmeerhaast.nl/txteng/the-book.html

Shelter
edited by Lloyd Kahn (Shelter Publications, 1973)

The Story of Mankind: A Picturesque Tale of Progress
Olive Beaupré Miller (The Book House for Children, 1963)

Tents: Architecture of the Nomads
Torvald Faegre (Anchor Press/Doubleday, 1979)

Web Sites

These two web sites are clearinghouses for yurt information. Look through the sites, and follow the links. There are hundreds of Mongolia- and *ger*-related links, but because the online information can change so quickly, I won't try to list them here. Begin with these.

www.CloudHouses.com
Author Dan Frank Kuehn's site

www.yurtinfo.org
The Yurt Foundation's many interesting links

homepage.mac.com/decthree/Menu11.html
David Cain, of Yestermorrow Design/Build School (www.yestermorrow.org) and his partner Nancy built, sewed, and assembled a 24-foot yurt from scratch and have now lived in it for the last three years in Vermont.

Sources

Most of my drawings of the miscelleaneous ancient *ger*-likc structures *(p. 1)* come with very limited documentation, but the similarities and variations are fascinating, even if we don't know exactly where or when the image or drawing was produced, or if the word associated with the image is the name of the structure, or the people, or in what language they call it that . . . Actually I was tempted to include a North American Mandan lodge with a very *ger*-like profile, as well as the classic dome of the Arctic Eskimo igloo, but they aren't really portable dwellings.

Shifting Boundaries—an exploration of natural building materials—is an exhibit which ran at the Mary E. Black Gallery in Halifax, Nova Scotia, Canada from May 13 to July 4, 1999 *(www.chbucto.ns.ca/culture/shifting_boundaries).*

PBS's Nature website for "Wild Horses of Mongolia with Julia Roberts," *(www.pbs.org/wnet/nature/mongolia)*

Photos of Peter and Jackie Main's trek across the Gobi with yaks and *gers* from their travel web site, *www.pbase.com/mr2c280/mongolia*

Torvald Faegre's *Tents. (See Further Research, Books, above.)*

Suppliers

The number of sources for yurt-related housing today is **huge**! These are a few interesting leads that have come my way. I hope I've covered the major makers. The range of styles is mind-boggling. I don't mean for this to be a complete compendium of what's out there, but an opportunity to revel in the variety.

No one paid for any plugs in the following pages, and in fact I can't endorse any of them, because I haven't used their products. The drawings come from images found in the makers' web sites. In some cases, a company makes only one yurt-like object, but often there are many more sizes and styles than you see here.

Ger Exporters/Importers

BioRegions International (non-profit corporation)
P.O. Box 6541
Bozeman, Montana 59771
Tel: 406-587-2406
info@bioregions.org
Web: www.bioregions.org

BioRegions International is a 501(c)3 non-profit organization that works to empower the nomadic cultures of Mongolia to survive in a rapidly changing world. They support holistic, locally-based projects promoting public health, education, environmental protection, and sustainable economic development. BioRegions International works closely with Montana State University and the semi-nomadic people of the Darhad Valley, northern Mongolia, to integrate research and community service. Projects are designed to support long-term solutions, cultural integrity, and cross-cultural understanding.

All proceeds from BioRegions' *ger* importation benefit local communities in Mongolia, directly funding projects with the semi-nomadic people of the Darhad Valley, northern Mongolia.

Bukhara Carpets
Furmanov Street 103 (corner with Aiteke-Bi), office 105
480091, Almaty, Kazakhstan
Tel/Fax: +7 3272 670510
cellular: +7 300 3209910 (Dmitriy)
cellular: +7 300 7333705 (Akul)
Email: info@bukhara-carpets.com
Web: www.bukhara-carpets.com/kazakh_yurt_for_sale.html

You may need a translator . . .

Silk Road Yurts
301-3608 7th Ave. West
Vancouver, B.C. Canada V6R 1W4
Tel: 604-537-6911
Email: simplify@silkroadyurts.com
Web: www.silkroadyurts.com

Silk Road Yurts imports genuine Mongolian yurts. Our yurts are available in a variety of sizes, and can be updated with windows at your request.

Traditional Builders in the UK

Albion Canvas Co
Unit 6, Barkingdon Business Park
Staverton
Totnes
Devon
TQ9 6AN
UK
Tel: 0845 456 9290 (local rate)
Fax: (0)1803 762734
International + 44 (0) 1803 762230
albioncanvas@yahoo.co.uk
Web: www.albioncanvas.co.uk

The Stunning Tents Company
7 Beech Hill Road, Spencers Wood, Reading
Berkshire, RG7 1HL
UK
Tel: 0118 988 2355
Fax: 0118 988 8306
Email: enquiries@stunningtents.co.uk
Web: www.stunningtents.co.uk/Yurt.html

Woodland Yurts
80 Coleridge Vale Road South
Clevedon
North Somerset
BS21 6PG
UK
Tel: 01275 879705
Web: www.woodlandyurts.freeserve.co.uk

Yurt Works
Greyhayes, St Breward
Bodmin
Cornwall
PL30 4LP
UK
Tel: 01208 850670
Web: www.coppiceworks.co.uk

Modern Yurt Design

Atelier des 3 Yourtes
Charles LEYS
6 rue des vergers
35 330 LES BRÛLAIS (Bretagne)
France
n°Siret: 444 189 328 00024
Tel/Fax: +33 (0)2 99 92 47 82
06 74 53 76 30
Email: charles@yourtes.fr
Web: www.yourtes.fr

Bruton Yurt Company
Jonathan & Caroline Morriss
The Barn
Higher Backway
Bruton
Somerset
BA10 0DW
UK
Workshop Tel: 01963 31955
Mobile Tel: 07710 210289
Email: byc@btinternet.com
Web: www.brutonyurts.com/home.html

The Colorado Yurt Company
P.O. Box 1626
Montrose, CO 81402
Toll-free: 800-288-3190
Tel: 970-240-2111
Fax: 970-240-2146
Web: www.advancecanvas.com

Great American Yurts
12233 Pendleton Pike
Indianapolis, IN 46236
Tel: 317-850-6785
Email: questions@yurts-r-us.com
Web: www.yurts-r-us.com

Living Shelter Crafts

P.O. Box 4779
Sedona, AZ 86340
USA
Fax: 928-204-1252
Web: www.aquarianconcepts.org/tipisyurts.html

Nomad Shelter Yurts

389 Grubstake #1
Homer, AK 99603
Tel: 907-235-0132
Email: nomadger@alaska.net
Web: www.nomadshelter.com

Pacific Yurts Inc.

77456 Hwy 99 South
Cottage Grove, OR 97424
Email: info@yurts.com
Tel: 541-942-9435
Fax: 541-942-0508
Web: www.yurts.com

Rainier Yurts

Rainier Industries, Ltd.
18435 Olympic Avenue S.
Seattle, WA 98188
Toll-free: 866-839-8787
Tel: 425-981-1253
Fax: 425-251-5065
Email: sales@RainierYurts.com
Web: www.rainieryurts.com

RS&M

P.O. Box 682
216 S Tower Road
Fergus Falls, MN 56514
Tel: 800-726-4028
Fax: 218-736-3216
Web: www.rsm-pvc-vinyl.com/yurts.htm

Steve Place and Francine Isaacs

Bont Glan Tanat
Llanrhaeadr Ym Mochnant, nr Oswestry, SY100AF.
Wales
Tel: 01691-780639
Email: steveplace@yurts.fsnet.co.uk
Web: www.yurts.fsnet.co.uk

The Alachigh used in the Caucasus Mountains, these tents are covered with felt like the yurt, but do away with the trellis walls.

Yurtco Manufacturing Inc.

Head Office
5784 Byrne Road
Burnaby, BC, Canada, V5J 3J4
Tel: 604-629-2982
Fax: 604-432-7404

US Office
433 Teller Road
Point Roberts, WA 98281
Tel: 866-498-7826 (866-4YU RTCO)
Email: info@yurtco.com
Web: www.yurtco.com

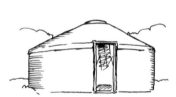

Yurt Source

6463 Highway 19 North
Dahlonega, GA 30533
Tel: 706-867-9446
Web: www.georgiamountaininn.com/getayurt.htm

The Yurt Workshop

Ratna & Rob
C/Naranjillos 16
Narila
Granada
18448
Spain
Tel: +34 958 76 81 21
Email: Info@YurtWorkshop.com
Web: www.yurtworkshop.com

Non–Nomadic Yurts

Alternative Buildings
Tel: 402-379-4974
Web: www.alternativebuildings.com

William Coperthwaite
The Yurt Foundation
Dickinsons Reach
Machiasport, ME 04655
Bill has no telephone.

Coperthwaite Yurt Designs
P.O. Box 183
Cambridge, Mass. U.S.A.

Goulburn Yurt Works
12 Copford Road Bradfordville Goulburn
P.O. Box 645 Goulburn NSW 2580
Australia
Tel: (02) 4821 5931
Fax: (02) 4821 6999
Web: site.yurtworks.com.au

Mandala Custom Homes
Toll-free: 866-352-5503
Tel: 250-352-5582
Fax: 250-352-0582
Factory: 1010-B 7th Street
Nelson, British Columbia
Canada
By Mail: Box 234
Nelson, BC V1L 5P9
Email: info@mandalahomes.com
Web: www.mandalahomes.com

Oregon Yurtworks, Inc.
1285 Wallis Street
Eugene, Oregon 97402
Tel: 541-343-5330
Toll-free: 800-211-8470
Fax: 541-344-0165
Email: info@yurtworks.com
Web: www.yurtworks.com

Yurt People
Vital Designs
P.O. Box 18
Talmage, California 95481
Tel: 888-225-9878 (888-CAL-YURT)
Web: www.yurtpeople.com/yurtpeople

Other Nomad Homes II

GeoLite Systems
6118 West 77th Street
Los Angeles, CA
Tel: 310-216-0410
Fax: 310-216-7614
Email: info.geolite@abac.com
Web: www.geolitesystems.com

Kifaru Shelter and Stove System
Kifaru International
4894 VanGordon Street
Wheat Ridge, CO 80033
Tel: 800-222-6139 or 303-278-9155
Mon.–Fri., 9:00 a.m. to 5:00 p.m., MST
Fax: 303-278-9248
Email: customerservice@kifaru.net

Made for hunters, these tipi-like tents have just one pole,
and a stovepipe that goes up through the center.

Nomadics Tipi Makers
17671 Snow Creek Road
Bend, OR 97701
Tel: 541-389-3980
Email: nomadics@tipi.com
Web: www.tipi.com

Rainbow Tipis
3/2 Brigantine Street
Byron Bay, NSW. 2480
Australia
Arts & Industry Estate
people.ozzienet.net/~rainbowtipis/home.htm
(look for "Bamboo Structures")

Red Sky Shelters
500 Merrimon Avenue
Asheville, NC 28804
Tel: 828-258-8417
Email: isis@redskyshelters.com
Web: www.RedSkyShelters.com

Reese Tipis, Inc.
2291-J Waynoka Road
Colorado Springs, CO 80915
Tel: 719-265-6519
Toll-free: 866-890-8474 (TIPI)
Fax: 719-265-1018
Email: info@reesetipis.com
Web: www.reesetipis.com

There are, of course, many other tipi-making businesses
around the world, large and small. Shop around!

Shelter Systems-OL
224 Walnut Street
Menlo Park, CA 94025
Tel: 650-323-6202
Fax: 650-323-1220
Email: shelter@best.com
Web: www.alaskatent.com

Southwest Nordic Center
P.O. Box 3212
Taos, NM 87571
Tel: 505-758-4761
Email: yurt@newmex.com
Web: www.southwestnordiccenter.com

The Southwest Nordic Center operates two separate winter backcountry yurt systems. There are four yurts at the southeastern end of the San Juan Mountains, near Cumbres Pass in southern Colorado, and one larger yurt above Taos Ski Valley in northern New Mexico.

Tentsmiths
P.O. Box 1748
Conway, NH 03818
Tel: 603-447- 2344
Fax: 603-447-1777
Web: www.tentsmiths.com

Worldflower Garden Domes
Worldflower Garden Domes
P.O. Box 2103
Georgetown, TX 78627
Tel: 512-431-9752
Web: www.gardendome.com

Cover material, dome kits & hubs.

Yurts in the System

Yurts are an option at some state parks in these states:

Alaska, Arizona, Arkansas, Colorado, Delaware, Florida, Georgia, Hawaii, Indiana, Iowa, Maryland, Massachusetts, Montana, Nevada, Ohio, Oregon, Pennsylvania, Rhode Island, Virginia, West Virginia, and Wyoming.

Washington State Parks

Idaho State University Outdoor Program
ISU Rental Center
Tel: 208-282-2945
Web: www.isu.edu/outdoor/yurt.html

Port Neuf Range Yurt

Bear Lake Yurt
Email: bearlakeyurt@yahoo.com
Web: www.bearlakeyurt.com

Center for Sustainability
College of Engineering
Pennsylvania State University
Web: www.psu.edu/dept/
cs/homestead.htm

I love yurt living. The yurt I live in at Penn State's Center for Sustainability is a Bill Coperthwaite design. He started the Yurt Foundation in Maine.

My yurt is completely powered by solar and wind energy. It has a radiant floor heating system that heats the whole structure evenly. The yurt has a polystyrene spray foam fill that completely seals the structure. The foam is sprayed into the wall and roof cavities—there are two walls and two roof gaps. The spray foam has R values near 45; awesome stuff! No off-gassing! Just last week we finished the living roof, which will help to keep the yurt cool in the summer, and add extra insulation in the winter.

I like my yurt because of its ground-hugging design. It deflects wind, rain, and snow away from the structure, which is particularly helpful in the tough snowy winter months. The ground-hugging design also makes the yurt hard to see until you're just about on top of it.

The yurt is the central structure in my renewable energy homestead, which has been funded by the Western Pennsylvania Sustainable Energy Fund. I'm researching ways of reducing ecological footprint and also developing a sustainability curriculum here at PSU."

–David Lettero, Manager

Luxury Extras II

Stoves

Elkhorn Stoves
20415 S. Patsy Drive
Oregon City OR 97045
Tel: 503-657-9215
Email: ervannmudder@msn.com
Web: www.elkhornstoves.com

New Energy Distributing
Vermont Castings
Tel: 800-852-1224
Web: www.newenergyinc.com/Products_htm/VC/aspen_wood_stove.htm

Pack Saddle Shop
3071 West Twin Road
Moscow, Idaho 83843
Tel: 208-882-1791
Email: support@packsaddleshop.com
Web: www.packsaddleshop.com
Follow the link to their Wall Tent Stoves—a great selection

Sims Stoves
312 Prickett Lane
Billings, Montana 59104
Tel: 800-736-5259
Email: simsstove@wtp.net
Web: www.wtp.net/simsstov

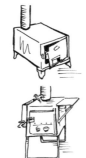

Wall Tent Shop
3071 West Twin Road
Moscow, Idaho 83843
Tel: 208-882-1791
Web: www.walltentshop.com

"France-Tulga" stove *(p. 79)* from

Zuunnaiman Suvraga Co.
Confederation of Mongolian Trade Unions' Building Room 312, 314, 317
Sukhbaatar Squire-2
Commercial Street-5
Ulaanbaatar
Mongolia
Post address #1: Box-957, Ulaanbaatar-13, Mongolia-211013
Post address #2: Box-140, Ulaanbaatar-51, Mongolia-211051
Tel: +976-11-320550, +976-11-319397
Fax: +976-11-314183
Email: 108suvraga@magicnet.mn
Web: www.108suvraga.mn/english/france_tulga.htm

Solar

Real Goods
13771 S. Highway 101
Hopland, CA 95449
Highway 101, just ½ mile south of Hopland
Tel: 707-744-2100
Fax: 707-744-1342
Web: www.realgoods.com

Ger with satellite dish and solar panel—in central Asia.

Tools & Materials

Cover Material

Nomadics Tipi Makers
17671 Snow Creek Road
Bend, OR 97701
Tel: 541-389-3980
Email: nomadics@tipi.com
Web: www.tipi.com/

Shelter Systems-OL
224 Walnut Street
Menlo Park, CA 94025
Tel: 650-323-6202
Fax: 650-323-1220
Email: shelter@best.com
Web: www.alaskatent.com/products/yard_goods.htm

Bamboo- and Woodworking Tools

Hida Tool, Inc.
1333 San Pablo Avenue
Berkeley, CA 94702
Tel: 510-524-3700
Toll-free: 800-443-5512
Web: www.hidatool.com

Coppicing

Living Countryside Ltd
Antrobus House
18 College Street
Petersfield
Hampshire
GU31 4AD
United Kingdom
Tel: 02392 410000
Web: www.coppicing.com

Thanks

I'd like to express my appreciation and affection, even, to all those who have helped me on my way, especially:

- To Sassafras, for the original yurt inspiration,
- To Bird and Non, for the transport of my poles and Everything,
- To Larry, Laurel, Rio, Ellie, Susan, Bruce, and all the others who let me camp on their land,
- To Rich, who let me cut poles in his backyard, and Daniel, and all the others who helped me gather poles,
- To Lawrence Ferlinghetti, for the title,
- To Nanao Sakaki, for use of his amazing poetry,
- To Jim Macey, for use of his wonderful photographs of Mongolian *gers*,
- To Ken Luboff, Noel Young, Ruth Gottstein, and Roger Yepsen, for their encouragement and advice,
- To Dennis, Harlan, Steph, Vito, Shalom, Harry, Seika, and Paul, for their invaluable assistance,
- And, to Susan for typing the first draft, to Barry for his Selectric typewriter, and Susanna for room to type.

Thanks, too, to all who encouraged me, and made space for me to work on the new edition:

- John & John, Kirk & Shelley, Evonne and everyone at MARS, the guys at the Jazz Club, Rick & Terry, Susanna & Juan, Mark & Torre, Todd & Laura, Mirabai & Gunga Das, Carl & Sharon, Bill Coperthwaite, Paul King for visiting the Mongolian *ger* builders, Paul Dembski for the author photos, and especially to Lew and Lloyd at Shelter for egging me on.

Thanks,
DAN FRANK KUEHN

About the Author

Paul Dembski

Dan Frank Kuehn grew up in the back of a North Dakota grocery store owned by his parents, Walter and Ann Kuehn. His father died in 1960, and Ann and her three sons, Jack, 13, Dan, 8, and Herb, 7, left the vast prairie for the relatively metropolitan Moorhead, Minnesota.

Dan graduated from Moorhead High School, and enrolled in a two-year course in commercial art at Moorhead Area Vocational Technical Institute. So much for formal education.

In the summer of 1970, Dan, 19, and his brother Herb, 18, floated 2,000 miles down the Missouri and Mississippi Rivers, from Bismarck, North Dakota to Memphis, Tennessee, searching for adventure.

After the trip commercial art no longer seemed like an attractive occupation, and after a few years of hitchhiking in the U.S. and Europe, Dan ended up in Taos, New Mexico in 1973, and was enchanted by both the place and people. He was hired on as janitor at a free school in Taos and worked there for three years.

He became interested in yurts and Mongolian culture in 1975, encouraged by the flourishing northern New Mexico alternative lifestyle scene. After many models and experiments, Dan spent a few years living in yurts he built himself (1976–1980), and completed the writing and drawing of the original *Mongolian Cloud Houses* in 1980.

Then Dan moved to Maui, Hawaii, and for 20 years he worked as a landscape designer. Native plant landscaping and garden guest house managing were his main occupations when along came the opportunity to revive his book on yurts.

He re-immersed himself in the subject. With the encouragement of his editors, Dan began an extensive rewrite to update the material and expand the scope of the book, with the addition of many new illustrations. *Mongolian Cloud Houses* is back, a romantic yet practical introduction to this ancient, elegant, nomadic dwelling.

Dan Frank Kuehn currently lives in Taos, New Mexico, designing advertising for artists and small businesses, as well as writing, teaching, and making strange noises.

Credits

Editor
Lew Lewandowski

Consulting Editor
Lloyd Kahn

Production Manager
Rick Gordon

Illustration and Handlettering
Dan Frank Kuehn

Typographic Design
Rick Gordon

Design Consultant
David Wills

Photo Credits
Cover: Melvyn Lawes / Corbis Corporation
104–110: Dan Frank Kuehn, Paul Dembski, Bruce Grossman, Terry Klein
111–120: Jim Macey
142: Paul Dembski

Proofreader
Robert Grenier

Printer
Courier Companies, Inc., Stoughton, MA

The back cover illustration is an old Russian lithograph of a yurt, previously published in *Shelter*.

The 1973 Classic

Shelter

edited by Lloyd Kahn

$24.95
11″ × 14½″
176 pages
ISBN-10: 0-936070-11-0

"How very fine it is to leaf through a 176-page book on architecture—and find no palaces, no pyramids or temples, no cathedrals, skyscrapers, Kremlins or Pentagons in sight . . . instead, a book of homes, habitations for human beings in all their infinite variety."
–Edward Abbey, *Natural History* magazine

"A piece of environmental drama."
–*Building Design* magazine

With over 1,000 photographs, *Shelter* is a classic celebrating the imagination, resourcefulness, and exuberance of human habitat. First published in 1973, it is not only a record of the countercultural builders of the 60's, but also of buildings all over the world. There is a history of shelter and the evolution of building types: tents, yurts, timber buildings, barns, small homes, domes, etc. There is a section on building materials, including heavy timber construction and stud framing, as well as stone, straw bale construction, adobe, plaster, and bamboo. There are interviews with builders and tips on recycled materials and wrecking. The spirit of the 60's counterculture is evident throughout the book, and the emphasis is on creating your own shelter (or space) with your own hands. A joyful, inspiring book.

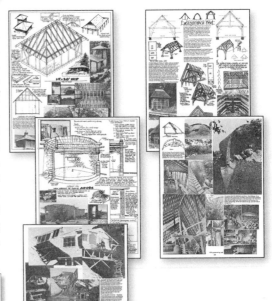

Shelter Publications
P. O. Box 279
Bolinas, CA 94924 U.S.A.
415-868-0280   1-800-307-0131 (orders)
orders@shelterpub.com   www.shelterpub.com

The Sequel to *Shelter*

Home Work
Handbuilt Shelter
by Lloyd Kahn

$26.95
9″ × 12″
256 pages
ISBN-10: 0-936070-33-1

"The book is delicious, soulful, elating, inspiring, courageous, compassionate . . ."
–Peter Nabokov, Chair, Dept. of World Arts and Cultures, UCLA

"Home Work *is a KNOCKOUT.*"
–John van der Zee, author of *Agony in the Garden*

". . . magnificent, invigorating, deep . . . and simply inspiring."
–Kevin Kelly, author; former executive editor, *Wired* magazine

Home Work, Lloyd Kahn's latest and most ambitious contribution to homemade architecture, a stunning sequel to *Shelter* that illustrates new and even more imaginative ways to put a roof over your head, some of which were inspired by *Shelter* itself. *Home Work* showcases the ultimate in human ingenuity, building construction and eco-centric lifestyle. What *Shelter* was to 60's counterculture, *Home Work* is to the Green Revolution, and more.

Page after page, *Home Work* describes homes built from the soul, inventiveness free from social constraint, but created with a solid understanding of natural materials, structure, and aesthetics. From yurts to caves to tree houses to tents, thatched houses, glass houses, nomadic homes, riverboats and more, each hand-built dwelling finds itself at one with its environment, blending harmoniously with the earth, using organically sustainable material.

Home Work features over 1,000 photos, including 300 line drawings, stories of real people building and living in their own houses, plus Kahn's recollections, reminiscences and observations gathered over the 30 years since *Shelter* was first published.

Shelter's New Book for Children

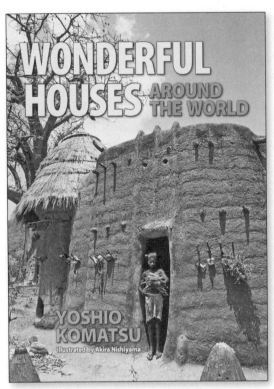

Wonderful Houses Around the World

by Yoshio Komatsu
illustrated by Akira Nishiyama

$8.95
7½″ × 10″
48 pages (paperback)
ISBN-10: 0-936070-34-X

$14.95
7½″ × 10″
48 pages (flexibound)
ISBN-10: 0-936070-35-8

"It's hard to imagine a better introduction to the variety of traditional house styles."
—Environmental Building News

A picture is worth a thousand words. The twelve photos in this book, along with the accompanying descriptive detailed drawings, make this a wonderful book for children. Photographer Yoshio Komatsu has travelled extensively around the world for 25 years, photographing handbuilt homes. There are photos of homes in Mongolia, China, Indonesia, India, Romania, Tunisia, Spain, Togo, Senegal, and Bolivia. Each structure is beautifully photographed, and then colorfully rendered in pen and watercolor, with many descriptive captions explaining the everyday life of children and families in these homes.

Yoshio Komatsu is a master photographer of people's dwellings, built of natural materials, from all over the world. The buildings he finds are wonderful and unique. Moreover, the people in the photos look relaxed and happy—obviously comfortable with the photographer. He has published several large books of his photos in Japan.